The Colors of
Catalonia

CIVIC CENTER

The Colors of Catalonia

In the Footsteps of Twentieth-Century Artists

VIRGINIE RAGUENAUD

GEMMA

BOSTON

First published by GemmaMedia in 2012.

GemmaMedia
230 Commercial Street
Boston, MA 02109 USA

www.gemmamedia.com

Printed in the United States of America

16 15 14 13 12 1 2 3 4 5

978-1-934848-83-8

Raguenaud, Virginie.
    The colors of Catalonia / Virginie Raguenaud.
        pages cm
    ISBN 978-1-934848-83-8 (pbk.)
1. Catalonia (Spain)—Description and travel. 2. Catalonia
(Spain)—In art. 3. Arts, Spanish—Spain—Catalonia—
20th century—Themes, motives. 4. Arts, French—France,
Southern—20th century—Themes, motives. I. Title.
    DP302.C61R35 2012
    914.67—dc23   2012013709

Cover design: Night & Day Design
Photographs courtesy of the author, except those
separately cited in the text.

Cover: André Derain, "Collioure Le Port de Peche," 1905
© 2012 Artists Rights Society (ARS), New York / ADAGP, Paris

To my two favorite artists, Sofiya and Natasha

CONTENTS

Introduction   1

CHAPTER 1   **The Wild Beasts**   5

*Henri Matisse and André Derain walk the old
cobblestone streets of* **Collioure**—*At the Fort St. Elme
with* Master and Commander *author Patrick
O'Brian—La Casa Quintana opens its doors for
acclaimed Spanish poet Antonio Machado—Polish
painter Willy Mucha hosts the Surrealist painter Max
Ernst—Sharing an apéritif with Pablo Picasso at Les
Templiers—Eating fresh sardines on the beach with
painters Louis Bausil and George-Daniel de Monfreid.*

CHAPTER 2   **A Sculptor, an Architect, and a
Revolutionary**   25

*A visit with sculptor Aristide Maillol in his home and
studio in* **Banyuls-sur-Mer**—*Visits with de Monfreid
and French painter Louis Valtat—Following in the
footsteps of architect and designer Charles Rennie
Mackintosh around the fishing port of* **Port-Vendres**
*to view his watercolors—Paul Gauguin's mysterious
adventures with the Spanish Revolutionaries in* **Cerbère**.

CHAPTER 3   **The Cult of Friendship**   55

Gatherings at George-Daniel de Monfreid's estate in
Corneilla-de-Conflent *at the foot of the Canigou
Mountain—The spirit of Paul Gauguin reigns—A visit
with Henri Matisse, Terrus, and Bausil—Exploring the
region with Gauguin's widow, Mette Sophie Gad—De
Monfreid and Gauguin's oldest son, Jean René, climb the
Canigou.*

Contents

CHAPTER 4   **The Mecca of Creativity**   79

*The Spanish Catalan sculptor Manolo Hugué makes
a home in* **Céret**, *French Catalonia—The cherry
blossoms and sunshine attract painters Juan Gris,
Chaim Soutine, Moise Kisling, and Marc Chagall—
The composer Déodat de Séverac discovers the Catalan
Cobla musicians—Evenings at the Grand Café with
"la bande à Picasso"—Picasso and Georges Braque rent
the Delcros home and develop Cubism—Gatherings at
Frank Burty Haviland's monastery, Les Capucins—
Salvador Dalí's grand entrance at the bullfighting
arena in 1965.*

CHAPTER 5   **Music, Monks, and Romanesque Art**   105

*A visit with Catalan painter Étienne Terrus, a
close friend of Henri Matisse, in* **Elne**, *the former
Episcopalian capital of French Catalonia—The young
Henry de Monfreid (George-Daniel de Monfreid's
son and future celebrated writer) and Jean René
Gauguin help stage an outdoor play—Front-row seats
at the international Pablo Casals music festival in*
Prades—*A tour of the Romanesque abbey of Saint
Michel de Cuxa—An inspired Raoul Dufy paints his
Orchestra series—Long nights of solitary writing for
Rudyard Kipling in* **Vernet-les-Bains**—*George-
Daniel de Monfreid's Le Calvaire watches over
worshippers at Notre-Dame du Paradis*

CHAPTER 6   **The Catalan Landscape**   129

Picasso's coming-of-age summer in **Horta de Sant
Joan**—*Reaching* **Gósol** *by mule with Picasso
and Fernande Olivier—Cubism and the Catalan
landscape—Surrealist painter Joan Miró discovers
country life in* **Mont-roig del Camp**—*A visit from
Miró's boxing partner, the writer Ernest Hemingway.*

CHAPTER 7   **The Surrealists on the Costa Brava**   163

*Salvador Dalí and his wife, Gala, entertain their
friends in* **Port Lligat** *and sail around* **Cadaqués**—
*Gatherings at Catalan painter Ramón Pitxot's house
with Pablo Picasso, Fernande Olivier, and André*

Contents

*Derain—**Figueres** and the spectacular Teatre-Museu*
Gala Salvador Dalí—Watching a bullfight with
Picasso, Eva Humbert, and Max Jacob—Exploring
*Casa-Museu Gala Dali, the medieval castle of **Púbol**.*

CHAPTER 8   **Sun, Sky, and Sand**   187
Spanish Catalan painters Santiago Rusiñol, Ramon
*Casas, and Miquel Utrillo in **Sitges** and the Catalan*
Modernisme movement—Picasso and his friend
Carles Casagemas's last visit with family before tragedy
strikes—Hiking along the crenellated towers and
*ramparts of **Tossa de Mar** in the footsteps of Marc*
Chagall and his "blue paradise."

Biographies   207

Bibliography   231

Acknowledgments   239

About the Author   241

INTRODUCTION

This book is about the inspiring intersection between art, travel, and the creative spirit. Together we will tour seventeen picturesque villages in French and Spanish Catalonia—places where some of the most brilliant minds of the art world found their courage and authenticity. In the fishing village of Collioure, Henri Matisse developed Fauvism with André Derain; Pablo Picasso matured as an artist in the mountain villages of Horta de Sant Joan and Gósol and later created Cubism with Georges Braque in Céret. Invigorated by the landscape around Cadaqués and Figueres, where he grew up, Salvador Dalí became the most famous of the Surrealist painters. Catalonia also welcomed Paul Gauguin, Charles Rennie Mackintosh, Joan Miró, Aristide Maillol, George-Daniel de Monfreid, Henri Manguin, Étienne Terrus, Louis Valtat, Marc Chagall, and many others. Some of these artists were natives of Catalonia, while others chose to pack up their suitcases and travel long hours by train to experience firsthand the glow of the Catalan landscape, its culture, and its people.

An important theme in this book is the power of travel on the creative mind. When you travel, you're confronted with a chance to expand your perspective, to grow, and to self-renew. You're out of the fog of your daily routines. When you allow yourself to be a stranger in a new place and invite the unknown into your life, you discover great things about yourself. When artists left Paris and arrived in Catalonia, they encountered a new language, a new landscape, and independent and self-reliant villagers who had their own rules and expectations. These artists were suddenly free from the pressures of the academic art world. The noise of the city had been left behind, and they could listen carefully to their own instincts and preferences and create authentic work. Most of the artists of the early twentieth century were guided by the most fearless traveler of them all, Paul Gauguin, who left Paris in 1891 to live among the inhabitants of Tahiti. They adhered to his call "to dare everything," and Catalonia proved to be the perfect place to unleash their creative spirits. I hope this book inspires readers to explore Catalonia and its sun-drenched villages, which stand tucked along the Mediterranean Sea or in the foothills of the Canigou Mountain.

Since traveling is like a good work of art, it's no surprise that many travelers also find refuge in art museums. As I walk along the halls of the Museum of Fine Arts in Boston, looking at how artists try to define the world around them, I'm immediately reassured that I too will find a way to make sense of the world around me. It's like a powerful walking meditation. There are treasures to be found not only in iconic art museums like the Louvre, the Musée d'Orsay, and the Hermitage, but also in smaller local museums. I hope this book motivates readers—whether they are on the road or at home—to learn more about the art and lives of both the great twentieth-century art pioneers and the lesser-known artists, including Étienne Terrus, George-Daniel de Monfreid, Gustave Fayet, and Louis Valtat, whose talent and vision greatly contributed to the development of modern art. I hope this book also reminds readers to support the arts in their local communities.

Maillol, Matisse, Miró, and many other artists struggled at the beginning of their careers. They often lacked the support of their families, who were unimpressed by their potential future as an *"artiste maudit,"* living the Bohemian lifestyle without any financial security. Still, they believed they had something worthwhile to contribute to their craft and persevered. I hope this book encourages artists—young and old—to believe in their work. As Gauguin declared in a letter to de Monfreid, "Criticism passes—good work remains."

Last but not least, a quick geography lesson. Catalonia was divided in 1659 by King Philip IV of Spain and King Louis XIV of France with the Treaty of the Pyrenees. The region was split along the Albères mountain range, which is part of the Pyrenees and forms a natural border between French and Spanish Catalonia. Spanish Catalonia is composed of four provinces: Barcelona, Girona, Tarragona, and Lleida. It covers an area of more than 12,000 square miles, and its capital is the city of Barcelona. French Catalonia includes six historical regions: Alta Cerdanya, Capcir, Conflent, Vallespir, Fenolheda, and Rosselló. French Catalonia is also known as the Roussillon or the *département* of the Pyrénées-Orientales. The region covers an area of 1,600 square miles, and Perpignan is the capital city. Strangely enough, because of miswording in the Treaty of the Pyrenees, there is one small Spanish enclave, the town of Llivia, which is still located in French Catalonia. After the signing of the treaty, many

Catalan villagers ignored the political and geographical developments, as they did not identify as either French or Spanish, but simply as Catalan. It was not until the French government came to the Roussillon to recruit soldiers during World War I that many villagers found out which country they were living in.

I hope you enjoy discovering the beauty of Catalonia and find inspiration in the colorful and uplifting personal stories of the great twentieth-century painters and writers who called it home, even if for just a summer.

CHAPTER 1

—~⁓⁓⁓~—

The Wild Beasts

Henri Matisse and André Derain walk the old cobblestone streets of
Collioure—*At the Fort St. Elme with* Master and Commander
*author Patrick O'Brian—La Casa Quintana opens its doors for
acclaimed Spanish poet Antonio Machado—Polish painter Willy
Mucha hosts the Surrealist painter Max Ernst—Sharing an apéritif
with Pablo Picasso at Les Templiers—Eating fresh sardines on the
beach with painters Louis Bausil and George-Daniel de Monfreid.*

View of the harbor and the church of
Notre-Dame-des-Anges in Collioure

Collioure

When Henri Matisse dropped his traveling gear, paint boxes, and easel at l'Hôtel de la Gare in Collioure in the spring of 1905, the artist had crippling doubts about his future as a painter. Matisse was then thirty-five years old with a law degree and three young children. He confided to his close friend and fellow painter Henri Manguin, "If I could, I would send painting to hell, it's scarcely satisfying and not lucrative enough." Matisse's father, disappointed by his son's lack of direction, had stopped giving him a monthly allowance, and Manguin had to lend him the money to make the trip to French Catalonia until his Parisian art dealer, Ambroise Vollard, could send him the few francs he was due. Unsure of his future, Matisse even applied for (and never heard back from) a job as a legal assistant to low-income families in Paris.

The now-legendary artist had an artistic breakthrough in Collioure. Was it sparked by the dramatic, sun-infused colors of the Côte Vermeille, the "Ruby Coast"? Or the well-timed friendships with free-spirited Catalan artists? Matisse indeed landed in the right location at the right time in his life, and, like any sensible traveler, he made the most of his journey.

In 1905, the village of Collioure was untouched by modernization. Tucked between the Pyrenees Mountains and the Mediterranean Sea, the old fishing village had three small, white beaches lined with over a hundred slender *catalanes* boats, painted in bright primary colors and displaying their distinctive inclined masts and tall, white triangular sails. The people lived a quiet and simple life, which revolved around fishing for sardines and anchovies. While the children ran through the labyrinth of narrow cobblestone streets and peeked through the doorways of pastel-colored homes, the women, dressed in black and wearing traditional bonnets, sat together near the beach mending fishing nets. The men napped in the shade, recuperating from another night of traversing the sea. From the end of April until the end of August, when the anchovy catch wound down, the fishermen set out to sea every evening with a bright light, or *lamporo*, attached to one end of their boats to attract schools of fish. By morning, families huddled on the beach to welcome the men home as they moored their crafts, their faces weathered by the forces of nature. Baskets overflowing with mackerels, sardines, and anchovies were wheeled to the market or sometimes sold right on the beach. Part of the catch was taken to the salting plants to be packed and exported.

Fishing was a family affair and the village's main occupation during the summer months. Collioure's twenty or so salting plants employed mostly women. As soon as boys reached puberty, their innocent childhood games of skipping rope and hopscotch came to a halt. They began training for a maritime life rehearsed for generations, hauling nets and raising sails with their fathers, uncles, and grandfathers at sea. At the beginning of the twentieth century, the Catalan villagers

The painter Henri Matisse at his easel
(Alvin Langdon Coburn, New York Public Library)

were self-sufficient and felt happily disconnected from the dealings of the French government in Paris. The train service, which had been in place since 1866, was still used mainly for commerce, and tourists were rare.

Matisse first heard tales about Collioure in 1904 during a summer visit to Paul Signac's home in Saint Tropez in southeastern France. The Pointillist painter had opened his villa's doors to Matisse and his wife, Amélie, and their three children—ten-year-old Marguerite (his daughter from a previous relationship), five-year-old Jean, and four-year-old Pierre. Signac had sailed to Collioure in 1887 and stayed long enough to splash color on four canvases. Intrigued by the brilliant light in these paintings, Matisse made the fateful pilgrimage to Collioure the following summer.

Upon his arrival, Matisse befriended Paul Soulier, a viticulturalist and art collector who lived next to the hotel. Matisse crossed paths with George-Daniel de Monfreid, who had been a close friend of the painter Paul Gauguin. De Monfreid often captained his yacht, *Le Follet,* bringing friends and family on trips along the Mediterranean coast. He is believed to be one of the earliest painters to immortalize Collioure, with a watercolor dated 1883. Matisse also connected with Étienne Terrus, a Catalan painter and vineyard owner who rode his bicycle to Collioure from his native village of Elne, eight miles away. It's easy to imagine Soulier, Terrus, and Matisse spending an afternoon with "The Captain," as de Monfreid was nicknamed, as he anchored his boat at the Boramar beach to discuss the day's sketches and share ideas for the best spots to paint *en plein air.*

As Matisse explored the quaint Moré district, the old part of town by the Boramar beach, his mind was full of impressions of the work of Paul Gauguin, Paul Cézanne, and Vincent Van Gogh. Although Cézanne was the only one still alive in 1905, each of these artists' audacity and autonomy appealed to Matisse's inquisitive state of mind. After years of studying at l'École des Beaux-Arts in Paris and countless hours spent copying the great masterpieces at the Louvre, Matisse wanted to create something new. Before he left Paris, Matisse had seen his friend Manguin's work on display, its pure color having taken over the canvas. Of one particular watercolor, we learn "[e]verything was blue…except the sky: the tree, the hill, the house, the sea." Matisse was captivated. As he later admitted, "I have never avoided the influence of others. I believe the personality of the artist develops and asserts itself through the struggles it has to go through when pitted against personalities."

In Collioure, Matisse spent long hours with Terrus questioning and analyzing different theories on art and the latest exhibits he had seen. He was searching to discover what was holding him back. Terrus was not afraid to engage. He voiced his opinions, argued, listened, and encouraged Matisse to break free from the Academy. In early July, Matisse was joined by another powerful ally—André Derain, a twenty-five-year-old French painter who was also eager to escape the trends in the French capital. Derain remembered with gratitude that Matisse had traveled to Chatou, on the outskirts of Paris, to convince Derain's father to let his son pursue his dream of becoming a painter. Derain was happy to accept Matisse's invitation to work alongside him in Collioure.

To Derain's surprise, Madame Rosette, the innkeeper, initially turned him down when he arrived at l'Hôtel de la Gare. As the inn's young helper, Mateu Muxart, later remembered, Derain stood in front of them that day like "a giant of sorts, skinny, all dressed in white, with a long and thin mustache, cat's eyes, and a red hat on his head." Madame Rosette demanded that Muxart throw him out, this man "dressed like a carnival." She was a grumpy old widow with a particular dislike of anyone who didn't speak Catalan, a language with Latin roots and a hint of old French mixed in. Her usual guests were railway workers or passing salesmen, but artists were a rarity. She had made an exception for Matisse because of the elegant disposition he projected, with his gold-rimmed glasses and clean suit. He had been quickly joined by his wife and their two young sons, which made the family man more respectable. Muxart persuaded Madame Rosette to give Derain a room in order not to insult their guest Matisse, who had won the inkeeper over with the helpful connections he had made with well-to-do locals.

As the summer of 1905 passed, Madame Rosette softened her approach toward Derain. The company who joined the artists for dinner at the hotel brought more business, which made Madame Rosette more pleasant. On August 4, a terrible storm hit Collioure and the painters were stuck indoors. To pass the time, Madame Rosette let Derain paint on the dining room door, but she mocked him in Catalan, as his bold choices seemed completely extravagant to her. The result was a life-size painting titled *Don Quixote and Sancho Panza*, which Soulier saved years later by taking down the door and replacing it with a new one. Unfortunately, the sketches that Derain hung in the dining room throughout the summer did not survive. As Muxart explained decades later, "Nobody told me they were worth more than calendars!" Poor Muxart was only fifteen years old that summer, and no one could have foreseen what those sketches would one day be worth.

Matisse rented his first studio on Rue de la Démocratie, overlooking the Port d'Avall, which was less a port than a wide, sandy beach. From his second-floor room, the artist studied the layout of the Faubourg district, guarded by the Tour de la Douane. He could see the medieval church of Notre Dame des Anges in the distance, its bell tower capped by a fanciful peach-colored dome. The iconic *clocher* is instantly recognized as the heart of Collioure and has been immortalized on canvases in museums around the world.

With his window open, Matisse painted the fresh geraniums on the wrought-iron balcony, the dark green shutters, and the colorful boats in the harbor beyond. Across the street, Derain set up his easel at the foot of the striking Château Royal—once the summer residence of the kings of Majorca—to paint *Le séchage des voiles*. From the wide footbridge that connects the Port d'Avall to the Boramar beach, he also painted *Port de Collioure—Le cheval blanc*. The iconic work's wide brushstrokes around white, untouched areas of primed canvas marked a monumental shift in early twentieth-century painting.

Matisse's and Derain's application of paint—sometimes laid directly on the canvas, instead of being mixed on the palette—was innovative, and their brave assortment of primary colors shook the art world. "I rejected everything on principle," wrote Matisse, "and followed my feelings, totally by means of color." Discovering Collioure at this particular phase of their artistic development completely liberated the two artists to create authentic work for the very first time. Derain described in a letter to the painter Maurice de Vlaminck, "[H]ere nothing is sad. The night is radiant, the day is powerful, ferocious, and triumphant. Lights scream out victory everywhere. It is not at all like the mists of the North, which are so compassionate to your misery." The painters' travels and their subsequent distance from the academic rules of the Parisian studios allowed them to paint with feeling. Matisse and Derain sketched and painted continually that summer in an attempt to capture the light, "Above all, the light. A blond light, a golden hue that suppresses the shadows," described Derain in a letter to Vlaminck. The painters imitated Collioure's bright colors under the fervent sun and unleashed their powers onto canvas, celebrating the daily activities of the townspeople. Matisse later wrote in his essay "Notes of a Painter," "We were like children in the face

The painter André Derain
(Agence Meurisse)

of nature and we let our temperaments speak." The artists absorbed their new surroundings and quickly succumbed to the intense colors. "There is no sky more blue in France than in Collioure," Matisse declared.

Matisse's and Derain's approach to nature was different from that of the trendy Impressionist painters who were taking over the most important and career-changing exhibition hall in Paris: the Salon d'Automne. As Matisse explained, "Nature is simply an opportunity for the artist to express himself... I wanted to create something out of my own experience... I wanted to see beyond [the Impressionists'] subtle gradations of tone... In short, I wanted to understand myself."

Although today nothing seems more joyful than a Matisse painting, when the world first became acquainted with the pure color art inaugurated by his stay in Collioure, viewers mocked the bold canvases. "This is madness!" exclaimed one guest at the Salon d'Automne in the fall of 1905, as he stood in front of *La femme au chapeau*. Another impromptu critic considered the works of Matisse and his friends to be "barbaric and naïve games of a child who is playing with the 'box of colors.'"

Louis Vauxcelles, the art critic reviewing the exposition for the Paris daily *Gil Blas*, surveyed the agitation of Room 7, where a simple marble statue of a young boy by sculptor Albert Marque was surrounded by large, colorful canvases from Matisse, Derain, Manguin, Vlaminck, Albert Marquet, and Georges Braque. Vauxcelles exclaimed, *"Donatello chez les fauves!"* or "Donatello with the wild beasts!" The initially pejorative name stuck, and Fauvism, the movement that defines the beginning of modern art, was born.

Matisse returned to Collioure in June 1906, but this time the family decided to settle for a longer stay. Matisse rented a home with a balcony overlooking the Boramar beach, as well as a studio adjacent to the Hôtel de la Gare, and Amélie registered their two boys at the local school. Classes were taught in French, although Pierre and Jean learned to communicate in Catalan with their classmates and with their local babysitter.

A typical morning for Matisse and his wife began around six with a walk to the nearby woods, which were dense with cork-oak trees overlooking the village. Here Amélie often posed in the nude, undisturbed. When the sun became too intense, Matisse packed up his notebooks, and the couple returned home for a swim in the ocean. At the time, the three Collioure beaches were strictly reserved for fishing activities, and the water was often dirty, so the Matisse family quickly adopted the Olla beach as their favorite swimming spot. They walked there from the Hôtel de la Gare, passing through a large tunnel and hugging the railway line until they reached a small path to the peaceful creek.

In mid-July they were joined for three weeks by the Fauvist painter Manguin, his wife, and their six-year-old son, Claude. The two friends had participated at the Salon des Indépendants in the spring, where Matisse displayed his extraordinary *Le bonheur de vivre*. The work came to be considered one of the most important paintings of the twentieth century and was purchased by the great avant-garde art collectors Leo and Gertrude Stein after the exhibition. The Stein family, which included their brother Michael and his wife Sarah, was developing a deep affinity for Matisse. They had already added *La femme au chapeau* to their bold collection, and they continued to encourage the artist, offering counsel and financial support. Sarah Stein would become the first collector to bring a Matisse painting to the United States, when she visited her hometown of San Francisco after the terrible earthquake of 1906.

Matisse had started the original sketches for his masterpiece *Le bonheur de vivre* during the previous summer on a property overlooking the secluded Olla beach, just north of Collioure's central bay. The site today belongs to the camping resort La Girelle and includes a small stone wall that runs alongside the beach. However, with a bit of imagination it is still possible to recognize *Le bonheur de vivre*'s heavenly site among the tall pine trees, with a touch of the Mediterranean Sea on the horizon.

During the summer of 1907, Matisse and Amélie crossed paths with de Monfreid, his wife and young daughter, and the Catalan painter Louis Bausil, who were enjoying the coast during a three-week vacation. De Monfreid would set up his easel in the morning by the Miradou fort overlooking the village and paint for a few hours. In the afternoon the group would swim or canoe from Olla beach to Collioure. They wrote letters to friends and visited with Terrus and Soulier. In the evening, sitting on the beach, de Monfreid and Bausil would "feast on sumptuous fresh sardines." On the eve of *la fête de Saint Jean*, "[t]he Matisses came to see us," noted de Monfreid in his journal, "and invited us to join them after dinner for a Saint John's bonfire." The summer celebrations were well under way in Collioure, but always interspersed with a few hours of painting.

*   *   *

When Matisse traveled back to Collioure in 1911, Pablo Picasso had made the nearby village of Céret his summer home, where he returned each year until World War I. Although Matisse and Picasso did not seek out each other's company, Picasso did occasionally travel the short distance to Collioure to share a *pastis* with fellow artists. He cheered and whistled at the bullfights in the arena east of the train station, where matadors skewered bulls (or vice versa) in the punishing afternoon sun. When he came back to Collioure in the 1950s, at the peak of his fame, Picasso stayed at the Hôtel des Templiers, owned by the Pous family, and spent his afternoons trading stories with fishermen at the bar. On August 14, 1953, Picasso signed René Pous's guestbook and sketched a bull. Pous proudly showed him his new thirty-foot wooden bar carved in the shape of a slender *catalane*, with a mermaid wearing a sailor's hat at the hull. By then Picasso had moved his primary residence to the Côte d'Azur, where his level of success brought intrusive media attention and a large group of hangers-on. Collioure provided a welcome refuge.

Every artist who found inspiration in Collioure left something behind on Les Templiers's walls to inspire visitors who might one day continue the creative circle. When visitors walk into the hotel at 12 Quai de l'Amirante, they are taken aback by the spontaneous museum that has spread over every wall, every room and every hallway of the three floors of the café, hotel and restaurant. The collection started in 1924 with a painting offered by the Russian artist Leopold Survage and expanded each time an artist made a "payment" for a warm meal. Paintings by French pointillist Henri Marre—who died in Collioure in 1927—and Dutch painter Augustin Hanicotte—who taught art to Collioure's school children for many years in the 1960s—hang over dark walnut tables where *joyeuses accolades* between friends fill the bar on Saturday nights. In the downstairs dining room, guests dine on paella with shrimp and a carafe of local red wine, surrounded by the collection's most modern works. Upstairs, displayed in a long glass case, a series of bowls and plates decorated with bullfighting scenes by Picasso captivate the attention of diners.

Les Templiers's guestbook, or *livre d'or*, has grown over the years into an exceptional document of Collioure's contribution to the arts. It catalogues signatures and sketches from Matisse, Czech painter Willy Mucha, Picasso, Survage, Juan Gris, George Braques, Marc Chagall, and many more. In 1948, Raoul Dufy, who was famous for having created the magical panel *La fée éléctricité* for exhibition at the 1937 World Fair in Paris, signed the book with a quick watercolor sketch of the Catalan fishing boats harbored on Collioure's Boramar beach. He added the poetic note, "*Collioure sans voiles, c'est un ciel sans étoiles*," or, "Collioure without sails is a sky without stars."

Hanging on the outside wall of Les Templiers is a large blue mosaic based on a drawing by Mucha. The Polish painter had discovered Collioure in 1940 and soon moved into an old stone home in the Moré district, determined to capture the rich nuances of the landscape in his paintings. As the

French writer Michel Déon once noted about Mucha, "Only uprooted individuals can grow such roots in our land and reveal to us, in their art, what we, too often, forget to see."

Over the years, Mucha and his wife entertained many guests in their three-storied house, including their close friend Dufy. In 1945, Mucha greeted the Surrealist painter Max Ernst and his wife, Dorothy Tanning, who spent fifteen days hiding out in Mucha's home from the journalists who had found out their whereabouts. Mucha and Ernst played chess on the large terrace of his studio, overlooking the *clocher*, and games of pétanque by the fig tree in the garden. When they parted ways, Mucha was moved by Ernst's desire to exchange paintings with him.

The owner of Les Templiers, René Pous, was a fervent supporter of the arts and tried to encourage all the artists who made Collioure their home, even if they only stayed for a short while. As Mucha said in an interview, "As soon as you mentioned you were an artist, no matter what medium, his table opened up." The *livre d'or*, kept in a safe by Pous's grandchildren, is worth its weight in gold, but the Pous family is more interested in preserving the past. Until he passed away in 2007, René's son, Jojo Pous, was known for generously letting (selected) guests peruse his treasured guestbook while giving them a personable art history lesson.

The Pous collection contains over two thousand artworks, although not all are on display. Some are being renovated, while others circulate at exhibitions around the world. Others are kept at a very discreet museum near the town of Auterive, on Route de Grépiac, south of Toulouse, where the Pous

Patrick O'Brian
(Julio Nayan)

Foundation keeps some of its most prized possessions. The museum is open only by special appointment and includes treasures such as a painting by Salvador Dalí done on silk, some of Matisse's famous paper collages from later in his life, drawings by Picasso, and paintings by Mucha, Lucien Maillol, and Dufy.

It was at Les Templiers that Picasso first met British writer Patrick O'Brian, a Collioure resident who would write the artist's biography some twenty years later. Both men enjoyed the tranquil Catalan way of life. O'Brian liked to hike on the outskirts of town where the Fort Saint Elme, a military look-out built in the sixteenth century, overlooks the entire bay. The site is so impressive that, in 1924, de Monfreid and his son Henry even inquired into buying the fort.

O'Brian's house hides on the rocky path called Chemin de St. Elme in the shadow of the fort. The shutters of his study are the only ones open in the home, as if to hint at a remnant of his presence, still sitting at his desk and creating the "best historical novels ever written," according to the *New York Times*. In this white stone house, O'Brian wrote his most famous work, a twenty-volume series describing the adventures of nineteenth-century Royal Navy member Jack Aubrey and mate Stephen Martin.

Born Richard Patrick Russ in Chalfont St. Peter, England, O'Brian changed his name after World War II to distance himself from his family. He left his wife and two children and started a new life with a woman named Mary Tolstoy-Miloslavsky. He often misled journalists and readers about his background, insisting that he was Irish and Catholic, and generally preferred to maintain a low profile.

When O'Brian settled in Collioure with his second wife in 1949, the weak French franc gave him an opportunity to stretch his British pounds, write, and survive. The couple's first apartment, on the third floor of 2 Rue Arago in the Moré district, had no hot water or electricity. But, as O'Brian observed, "If you're poor, you might as well be poor in a warm country." Thanks to the generosity and hospitality of their Catalan neighbors, the O'Brians often discovered wrapped-up sardines, garden vegetables, or a bottle of red wine from a local family's *cellier* on their doorstep.

In 1955, after some success in publishing, O'Brian was able to build the white stone house on Chemin de St. Elme. The house was originally a simple *casot*, or winegrower's house, stuck on a steep incline. The only neighbors at the time were grapefruit and lemon trees and wide vineyard terraces cascading down the mountain. In the 1970s and '80s, how-ever, residential buildings sprouted up all around, many taller than O'Brian's house and overlooking his garden. To quell his growing frustration, O'Brian hired a helicopter to fly over the property and drop a hedge of cypress trees to plant in the yard and restore his sense of privacy. O'Brian was named a Commander of the British Empire by the Queen of England and passed away in January 2000. He is buried at his wife's side in Collioure's cemetery, La Croette, on the outskirts of town, overlooking the bay.

His stepson, Count Nikolai Tolstoy (Mary's son from a previous marriage), now owns the home and visits Collioure with his family a few times a year. Nikolai, a distant cousin of the Russian writer Leo Tolstoy, published the first volume of a biography of O'Brian in 2004.

In 1939, Collioure provided a safe haven to the revered poet Antonio Machado, as he arrived exhausted after a long and difficult exile from Spain. Machado fled Madrid with his mother during the Civil War and arrived at the Villa Quin-tana, where he was comforted and looked after by the inn's owners. The house, near the bustling market on Place du Maréchal Leclerc, stands at 2 Rue Antonio Machado and currently serves as a museum and cultural center promoting Spanish literature. Machado passed away on February 22, 1939, just a few months after his arrival in Collioure. He is buried with his mother in the town's oldest cemetery, on Rue du Jardin Navarro. His grave site is consistently covered with fresh flowers and contains a glass jar filled with letters and poems written by fans from around the world.

Contemporary artists continue to be inspired by the extraordinary setting and warm Catalan spirit of this colorful town of 2,900 people (swelling to 10,000 in the summer). The region's traditional culture is apparent in the details— from the nautical lampposts and the road signs written in Catalan to the century-old anchovy plants and the long afternoon games of *pétanque* in the town square. Folklore festivals are organized around the mesmerizing circle dance called the *sardana*, with its traditional red-and-white costumes and rapid footwork. With their fingers intertwined, their arms raised high, and espadrilles on their feet, the dancers keep pace with the Cobla orchestra. The musicians play captivating rhythms with regional instruments like the *labiol* (a small flute), the *tenora* and *tible* (rustic oboes), and the *tombori* (a very small drum).

In order to preserve its proud heritage in this brilliant, amphitheater-like landscape, the town implemented strict development laws in 1989, and Collioure was eventually declared a national landmark. In spite of overcrowding and parking problems during July and August and the disappearance of almost all maritime activity, Collioure still promises a peaceful Mediterranean way of life. As the locals like to say in Catalan, "*A Cotlliure, hi fa bon viure!*" Yes, life is good in Collioure.

CHAPTER 2

A Sculptor, an Architect, and a Revolutionary

A visit with sculptor Aristide Maillol in his home and studio in **Banyuls-sur-Mer**—*Visits with de Monfreid and French painter Louis Valtat*—*Following in the footsteps of architect and designer Charles Rennie Mackintosh around the fishing port of* **Port-Vendres** *to view his watercolors*—*Paul Gauguin's mysterious adventures with the Spanish Revolutionaries in* **Cerbère***.*

Aristide Maillol in his studio
(Alfred Kuhn)

Banyuls-sur-Mer

One evening during the peak of his career, Auguste Rodin visited the art dealer Ambroise Vollard in Paris. Throughout dinner the famous sculptor stared at a small statue by Aristide Maillol prominently displayed above the fireplace. As Vollard recounted in his memoirs,

> "Rodin's presence led us naturally to talk of sculpture.
> — 'If we hadn't got *you*, Master,' declared someone, 'sculpture to-day…'
> — 'And what about *him*?' retorted Rodin, pointing to the Maillol."

Indeed, when Rodin passed away in 1917, European art critics immediately looked to Maillol as the next great sculptor of the time.

However, Aristide Maillol did not begin his career as a sculptor. Having executed his first landscape at the age of thirteen, in his hometown of Banyuls-sur-Mer, Maillol initially wanted to become a painter. His aunt, who had raised him from birth when his mother abandoned him, tried to support him with her limited means. After repeatedly taking the entrance exams, he finally joined the Ecole des Beaux Arts and at age twenty left his native Catalonia for Paris. The artist lived in utter poverty during those years and at times was so severely undernourished that he required medical care. But his determination was intact.

When Maillol returned to Banyuls in 1893, he was on a new creative course. Through his friendship with an engaging group of artists called Les Nabis (meaning "prophet" in Hebrew), Maillol had been encouraged to experiment with different mediums and had discovered the art of tapestry design. Les Nabis was formed in 1888 and included, among others, the painters Eduard Vuillard, Pierre Bonnard, and Maurice Denis, and the poet Marc Lafargue. The group was united by its members' complete distrust of the academic arena and by the creative sentiment that no one art medium was superior to any other. The artists found it vital to express themselves through decorative arts such as ceramics and textiles in addition to fine arts such as painting and photography. Maillol was drawn to the freedom and authenticity of their approach, which were reminiscent of the values he had grown up with in French Catalonia.

Upon his return to his aunt's *maison rose* or "pink house," as it is now referred to in the village, Maillol opened a tapestry workshop with the help of two young employees, Angélique and Clothilde Narcisse. Together they worked diligently to prepare for the important 1894 Salon de la Libre Esthétique taking place in Brussels. Paul Gauguin, who himself had five paintings on display at the avant-garde show, praised Maillol's tapestries and encouraged him to continue his work. The public agreed. Princess Marthe Bibesco, a well-known Romanian-French writer, immediately ordered two tapestries.

Maillol's newfound clients were impressed by his technical skills and his insistence on using traditional natural pigments to dye his thread. Maillol often walked around Banyuls in the foothills of the Pyrenees Mountains, looking for plants such as the common madder, which is known for three-foot-long roots that produce a beautiful red dye. True to his upbringing, Maillol rejected the artificial and the superficial, in both his work and his personal relationships.

Maillol soon fell in love with Clothilde Narcisse and the two were married in Banyuls in July 1896. As a wedding present, Paul Gauguin gave the young couple a painting titled *Misères humaines* (Human misery). Gauguin had either a peculiar sense of humor or a low regard for the institution of marriage!

Like many young artists of his generation, Maillol recognized Gauguin as a powerful force of inspiration. "He understood the importance of [Gauguin's] message," wrote Dina Vierny, the last model to work with Maillol. She believed the future sculptor and his fellow artists thought of Gauguin "as a king, as a wizard, as a magician!" In April 1899, Gauguin— who had described Maillol as a "soul of gold"—inquired from Tahiti in a letter to his friend George-Daniel de Monfreid, "Does [Maillol] still make masterpieces in tapestry?" Unfortunately, Maillol was by then struggling with his eyesight. He was eventually forced to give up the intense and meticulous work of tapestry design.

Before closing his tapestry workshop, Maillol had befriended the French painter Louis Valtat, who dropped by to see his work. In the mid-1890s, Valtat was fighting tuberculosis and had been advised by doctors to recuperate under the warm Mediterranean sun with an abundance of fresh air. He visited Collioure and Banyuls as well as the health resort of Vernet-les-Bains, where he met the painter George-Daniel de Monfreid. In the presence of Maillol and de Monfreid, Valtat was initiated to Gauguin's decorative art and began "to explore the expressive potential of pure colour long before the famous Salon d'Automne of 1905." His 1896 painting, *Les barques sur la grève,* for example, showcased Valtat's avant-garde preference to omit certain impressions and to focus instead on the emotional response to nature created with his "dancing brushwork." As the art historian Albert Kostenevich wrote, Valtat "was consumed by a desire to paint with absolutely unmixed, bright colours."

His work had an undeniable influence on Matisse's Fauvist paintings completed in Collioure. Before Matisse traveled south in May 1905, he had the chance to study Valtat's work, exhibited by their mutual art dealer Vollard. As a nod to Valtat's importance in the development of modern art, his exhibition titled Vue Méditerrannéene ("Mediterranean landscape") came between Gauguin's exhibit in November 1903 and Matisse's exhibit in June 1904.

When his health permitted it, Valtat traveled with Maillol and de Monfreid throughout Catalonia. They traveled by train to Cerbère, Figueres, and Llançà, sometimes opting to ride their bikes. "Valtat is in rapture," noted de Monfreid during one of their excursions. Valtat also witnessed de Monfreid's and Maillol's first sculpture attempts in 1897. On January 21, the three friends had dinner together in Banyuls, when de Monfreid decided "to stay with Valtat and Maillol until tomorrow, as the latter must empty the kiln this afternoon." With the support of his friends, Maillol had begun to model small terracotta figurines and statuettes in clay.

From a studio in the basement of his aunt's house, which he would eventually inherit, Maillol also enjoyed carving small statues from the soft wood of the pear and olive trees that grew on the outskirts of Banyuls. On occasion, he would leave his "cave," as he called it, to work outside in the front garden, shaded by a large pine tree. Seeing his friend develop an interest in sculpture, de Monfreid, who lived in nearby Corneilla-de-Conflent, convinced Maillol to visit an exhibit featuring more of Gauguin's artwork and sculptures at the Café Volpini in 1899, during the World Fair in Paris. The work Gauguin was producing in Tahiti, including carvings in relief from the 1890s such as *Femme aux mangues* and *Soyez mystérieuses* deeply affected Maillol.

The Catalan sculptor almost always used the female body as his inspiration, and eventually turned to large figures. With confidence, he simplified the lines of his models, smoothed out their skin, and quieted down their expressions—a significant shift from Rodin's emotive and complex statues. During an exhibit of Maillol's early sculptures, Rodin was smitten with a statue titled *Léda*, declaring, "I don't know in all of modern sculpture a piece that is as categorically beautiful as Léda, as categorically a masterpiece."

Throughout his career, Maillol served as the link between Paris and French Catalonia, enticing artists to travel south and discover the beautiful seaside village on the Côte Vermeille.

The first thing Maillol's friends noticed upon arriving—as visitors do today—was the town's luminosity. Banyuls simply glows. The harbor is divided into two large coves, one crowded with large and small pleasure boats and the other ready to welcome swimmers and windsurfers. Protected by the Pyrenees mountain range, the villagers attend to the miles and miles of terraced vineyards that rise above the town and produce the world-renowned Banyuls wine.

As I sit here drinking a glass, I think of my grandfather, who managed his own vineyard and introduced me to the sweet wine. He would offer it in a small glass, usually as an apéritif, although many people also drink it as a dessert wine, to celebrate the family coming together. Everyone cheered "*A votre santé!*" wishing for good health and happy times ahead. I remember my grandfather telling us that it was the Knights Templar—an intriguing group of religious warriors who were, among other things, savvy businessmen—who had pioneered the distillation process of the Banyuls wine back in the thirteenth century. Today, in the underground cave of their castle, Mas Reig, visitors to Banyuls can revel in the mysterious atmosphere of the place where more than five hundred oak barrels are stored during the long fermentation process. Depending on the type of wine—sweet, medium-dry, or *rancio*—the barrels are kept underground or placed outside under the scorching summer sun and cold winter weather for two to four years. During fermentation, the Banyuls wine is fortified with double-distilled *eau de vie* grape spirit, which gives it its unique aroma.

When Maillol invited fellow artists to his home, the drink

of choice was often the *rancio* Banyuls wine served with cheese and bread. The sculptor enjoyed sharing the local produce that found its way onto his kitchen table, like the Banyuls wine vinegar and olive oil, the green and black olives, the figs, and the popular honey used in many local recipes. On May 22, 1905, Clothilde and Maillol were ready to set up the table once more, this time for a get-together with their good friend Étienne Terrus, in honor of the newly arrived Henri Matisse.

Unfortunately, the other guests—de Monfreid, the Catalan painter Louis Bausil, and Fernand Dumas, a Perpignan banker and generous art collector—arrived late because of car trouble. To make up for the disappointment, de Monfreid invited everyone to his estate in Corneilla-de-Conflent on June 12 for lunch to continue the conversation. De Monfreid was eager to share his Gauguin treasures with Matisse.

In a letter to his friend, the painter Albert Marquet, Matisse recounted his visit with Maillol. "We went to see, (led by Terrus), the sculptor Maillol who was working on a statue twice its natural size, and since I saw him struggling with the molding, I helped him for two days. I did not mind because, in addition to getting to know him more personally, the statue is lovely. The weather was dreadful for those two days, the rain came down in buckets." Matisse himself had begun sculpting since 1900 and enjoyed exploring the medium.

Maillol revealed the sculpture *La Méditerranée* at the famous 1905 Salon d'Automne, in a room adjacent to Matisse's and Derain's colorful artwork from Collioure. When the piece debuted, the *coup de foudre* by the public and the critics was immediate. *La Méditerranée* was seen as "[t]he first statue that breaks off with sculptural Impressionism, and finds in the plastic arts this pure form, announcing a new path, the cradle to twentieth century sculpture." Maillol had found his way. The wealthy art collector Count Kessler of Germany, whom Maillol had the good fortune to meet in 1903, admired his sculptures and soon became his lifelong *mécène*, or patron, freeing the artist from financial worries.

When Maillol returned to Banyuls from his trips to Paris, the Catalan artist often walked the streets of Banyuls with a notebook tucked in his pocket, looking for inspiration. Wearing a traditional *barretina* wool cap and black espadrilles, Maillol would leave his house perched in the Cap Doume quarter and walk down the large stone steps to the bustling port below, his long beard still littered with pieces of plaster from the morning's activity. He would watch the fishermen unloading crates, or a game of *pétanque* on the square, or children filing out of the bakery. He stopped to make quick sketches of young girls giggling in secrecy, noting their gestures, the detail of an ankle or a pretty movement of the head. "Move along!" a disapproving passerby would say, surprising Maillol in his reverie. One afternoon while sitting at a café, Maillol and a friend from Paris watched a girl "with a fine, generously molded figure" pass in front of them. His blue eyes coming to life, Maillol quipped, "I have often been rebuked for not making my women slender enough. Now you see! I sculpt the women of my country!"

Maillol sometimes continued his walks along the rocky coves in order to admire the lighthouse a few miles out on

Cap Béar. He would then carefully thread the path along the vertiginous cliffs to the outskirts of town to sketch the young women working in the vineyards. "It is the most beautiful scenery in the world," the Catalan native wrote.

In his later years Maillol also enjoyed sketching details of the many tropical plants that had been brought to Banyuls in the 1870s by Napoleon III's personal gardener, the botanist Charles Naudin. Naudin had owned a home called Villa Palma in nearby Collioure, whose remaining tropical gardens greatly influenced Henri Matisse during his stay in Catalonia. As in Collioure and many other villages along the coast, the Mediterranean climate and sheltered harbors were conducive to growing eucalyptus, yellow-flowered cactus, magnolias, pomegranates, and palm trees. These palms line the main road in Banyuls, now called the Allée Maillol, where Maillol's statue *La jeune fille allongée* is on display. To counter the academic tendencies of the time, Maillol insisted that all his statues and monuments be presented at eye level instead of on traditional pedestals.

In 1910, as Vollard sold more of his statues from Paris, Maillol was able to buy a small farmhouse a few miles southwest of Banyuls, along the Baillaury Valley. Maillol enjoyed the walk from the pink house in the center of Banyuls to the "Métairie Maillol," as it was soon nicknamed. However, for the occasional out-of-town visitor who might venture out of the sheltered harbor during a harsh northwest wind, the experience was quite different. The *tramontana* ("across the mountains") wind is famous for its sweeping force that chases away the clouds, clears the air, and brings in exceptional sunshine.

Unfortunately only the locals seem to become accustomed to it. In his memoirs, Vollard recalled one of his messengers telling him with great agitation upon his return to Paris, "I did not find Mr. Maillol at Banyuls itself. I had to go five kilometers beyond it to dig him out at his farm; five kilometers that I had to do bent double, almost on all fours, not to be carried up into the air!"

The *tramontana* wind can change destinies. When the sculptor Manolo Hugué and the painter Frank Burty Haviland came down from Paris in 1909, looking for a warm and inexpensive place to renew their creativity, they considered settling in Banyuls-sur-Mer. As the story goes, they were quickly discouraged by the tempestuous wind and kept hiking, eventually dropping their bags down in calmer Céret, where another chapter of modern art history was about to unfold.

Maillol's studio in the old farmhouse provided peace and quiet for the artist. As he listened to music on his phonograph, Maillol read, painted, and studied his preparatory drawings as a new order of statues came in. "The farmhouse saved me," he once revealed. In photographs taken at the farm, he looks somewhat melancholic, but his lonely childhood, his mother's inability to nurture him, and his father's early death were heavy burdens to bear. He liked to meditate before working, a habit his friend Matisse picked up later, and he preferred to work alone, sometimes outside under a rustic veranda to protect himself from the harsh sun. He kept a simple lifestyle and was always a bit thrifty, perhaps remembering the difficult early days in Paris.

The Impressionist painter Pierre-Auguste Renoir, who was

enjoying worldwide recognition, began sculpting at the end of his life and had seen Maillol at work. As he described to their mutual dealer, Vollard, "I found [Maillol] in his garden, hammer and chisel in hand, before a block of stone. So many modern sculptors merely plagiarize the ancients, but Maillol is such a true descendant of the Masters, that as I watched him disengaging his forms I was reminded of a Greek. I caught myself looking for the olive trees." The encounter must have happened at his studio outside Paris, where Maillol lived for part of the year—had he been in Catalonia, Renoir truly would have seen the olive branches all around him.

One can imagine Maillol at work by looking at the beautiful painting done by his friend Edouard Vuillard, titled *Portrait of Maillol*. The work was completed in the early 1930s and shows the artist sculpting in his garden, wearing an orange-striped suit and a straw hat and putting the finishing touches on his monument to Cézanne. It is a touching tribute to the artist and reminds us that Maillol had a strong group of dedicated and loyal friends who admired his work and successfully petitioned for him to win certain government commissions, greatly adding to his legacy. Maillol received an order for a sculpture to honor the French politician Auguste Blanqui, which he titled *L'action enchaînée*. He also completed important war memorials, which can be seen today in the Catalan towns of Elne, Port-Vendres, Banyuls, and Céret.

Maillol had creative bursts away from sculpting as well. On one occasion, when Matisse approached the farmhouse expecting to find the artist hard at work on one of his commissions, he instead discovered Maillol chewing with great gusto as he paced around his studio. Curious, Matisse inquired as to what the artist was doing, prompting Maillol to grab the white ball in his mouth and smash it flat on the wall. With great pride, he exclaimed, "Here is my future paper custom made. I can get it by turning white cotton into a paste!" Sure enough, by 1913, with the financial backing of Count Kessler, Maillol was in the mill business producing precisely the sheets of paper he needed for his drawings. Maillol designed a particular watermark of a nude encircled with a ribbon for the paper, which he named Vergé de Montval. This watermark has been found on the drawings of Matisse and Picasso. Although the business was eventually sold to another company, the Montval paper still exists today.

During the extended stays he made in Collioure from 1905 until 1914, Matisse often traveled to Banyuls to visit Maillol, and the two became close friends. The sculptor's work ethic and his kind and humble demeanor left a strong impression on Matisse, so much so that when Matisse's son Jean discovered an interest in sculpting in the early 1940s, he advised him to study with Maillol. Thus, like the Catalan artist himself, Jean began creating delicate nudes carved from eucalyptus wood.

The fact that Maillol did not establish himself as a sculptor until the age of forty leads budding artists to sympathize with the man and feel considerably more hopeful. Similarly, his good friend Matisse was thirty-five years old before he had his major breakthrough. With age came wisdom, as Maillol later reflected, "I'm enjoying myself, nothing is eternal... Art for me doesn't have this serious, this terrible importance that it has for the members of the Institute. If one screws up a piece, one doesn't kill himself, one simply makes another one." Nevertheless, Maillol had forty years of glory. As his model Vierny noted, "His life changed considerably but his mannerisms and his day-to-day life didn't change too much. He focused on his work."

In a strange and dark twist, Vollard, who had taken a chance on the sculptor at the beginning of his career, remained connected to Maillol even in death. In 1939, as Vollard was traveling by car as a passenger, an accident occurred and one of Maillol's statues, which had been resting on the back shelf, knocked Vollard in the back of the head and killed him instantly. Maillol also lost his life in an automobile accident, five years later. As the artist rode in the passenger seat on his way to visit the painter Raoul Dufy in nearby Vernet-les-Bains, the car veered off the road during a rainstorm and crashed. Maillol succumbed to his injuries a few days later. He is buried in the quiet garden of his beloved farmhouse with a bronze casting of *La Méditerranée* watching over him from above his grave.

Port-Vendres

Our childhood summers in Catalonia always included a trip to Port-Vendres. We had heard countless times from our grandmother that, sadly, Collioure's fishing traditions had disappeared forever and that now all the good anchovies were

View of Port-Vendres and the church of
Notre-Dame-de-Bonne-Nouvelle

in Port-Vendres. As French Catalonia's only deep-water port able to accommodate 500-foot-long vessels, Port-Vendres is a true working harbor. Cargo ships maneuver the waters to the shore to unload over 220,000 tons of fruits during the course of the year. Large, elegant yachts share the inner basin with fishermen in their *lamparos* coming back to shore with barrels of sardines, anchovies, and crayfish. As children we would go to the wharf and listen to La Criée, the professionals-only fishing market, where the auctionneer's voice kept us laughing for days. There's an expression in French for someone who is obnoxiously loud, particularly when they are giving out orders to others: *"Quelle voix de poissonnière!"* Although it never feels good to be on the receiving end of this saying, in Port-Vendres, it's just business as usual. Rest assured, you don't have to own a restaurant or a grocery store to access the catch of the day. There is a shop behind the fish market and a popular bar and restaurant where you can enjoy a tasting of oysters, shrimp, crabs, and other *fruits de mer* with a glass of white wine.

When the Scottish architect, furniture designer, and painter Charles Rennie Mackintosh settled in Port-Vendres during the winter of 1925, the port welcomed cargo ships from North Africa, particularly Algeria. France and Algeria traded in everything from copper, timber, machinery, cattle, and sheep to cereal, dairy products, wine, fruits, and vegetables. As the closest French port to Africa, the town advertised twice-weekly passenger ships, which transported over 100,000 people every year. Matisse came to Port-Vendres in May 1906 to take advantage of the ferry service. He and his wife, Amélie, made the twenty-two-hour boat trip to Algiers, where they vacationed for two weeks. While in Algeria, Matisse traveled to Constantine, Batna, and Biskra. He returned with a canvas, entitled *Biskra Street,* and beautiful textiles and potteries that he would later include in his paintings. Today, cruise ships can often be seen in the harbor, their countries of origin denoted by a wide range of international flags.

Mackintosh and his wife, Margaret MacDonald, also a prominent artist of the Arts and Crafts movement, often watched this whirlwind of activity in the port from their second-floor balcony at the Hôtel du Commerce on the Quai Pierre Jorgas. The perfectly situated hotel was owned by the family Dejean. The Dejeans grew fond of the couple, who were regular patrons of the establishment until 1927, when Mackintosh was forced to return to England for medical reasons.

The discreet couple made a habit of walking to the wharf after dinner, sometimes continuing to the old port. There they could admire the marbled obelisk built for King Louis XVI in the eighteenth century and Maillol's nearby war memorial representing Venus handing a palm to the honored soldiers of World War I. This statue is a fitting masterpiece for the town, as its name is derived from the Latin *Portus Veneris* or "Port of Venus."

In addition to the bustle of the fishing and commercial industries, the couple witnessed the military activity of the naval port. Mackintosh reported one morning, "A Squadron has arrived today about 11 o'clock quite unexpectedly—3 big battleships outside the mole—and torpedo boats and other craft in the harbor." Because of its strategic location, the port had been fortified during the seventeenth century by King Louis XIV's chief military architect, Vauban.

Port-Vendres offered (and still offers) many idyllic spots

to paint *en plein air*. As the couple finished a bottle of red wine with the evening's last dish of fruit and cheese, Mackintosh pondered where to set up his easel the next morning. By the brick lighthouse at the Fanal Redoubt at the entrance of the port? By the blue-dome Roman-Byzantine church of Notre Dame de Bonne Nouvelle? Mackintosh sometimes settled with his paints and easel by the army forts or by the Cap Béar lighthouse on the outskirts of Port-Vendres. Perched more than 250 feet above sea level, the lighthouse was built in 1905 out of pink marble excavated from a quarry in Villefranche-de-Conflent.

These were the final years of Mackintosh's life, and he was content to lead a quiet existence in the south of France, focusing solely on his painting. As his wife described in a letter to a friend back in Glasgow, the couple wanted to linger in "this lovely rose-coloured land...glad to be back again in its warmth and sun." The Mackintoshes had first explored French Catalonia in 1923, spending a few months in Amélie-les-Bains, Céret, and Collioure. Now they were back for good, for what they would describe as the happiest years of their lives.

As an architect, Mackintosh had pioneered a new style of design in Scotland. His legacy is showcased as a permanent exhibition around Glasgow with the support of the School of Art, the Hill House, the Mackintosh House, and the House for an Art Lover, as well as the Willow Tea Rooms and several private homes. He combined the Art Nouveau philosophy with the clean, simple lines of Japanese art and added

Scottish Arts & Crafts designer and watercolor
painter Charles Rennie Mackintosh

a touch of his own Scottish heritage. Although he lived in
relative obscurity in his home country, Mackintosh was celebrated throughout Europe, especially in Germany and Aus-
tria. Today he is considered a pioneer of modern design.

Mackintosh often incorporated floral-inspired decorative
motifs into his furniture, and these eventually found their
way into his paintings as well. Mackintosh was "[f]ascinated
by the organic structures of geology and botany," which suggests that he might have become great friends with his neighbor Aristide Maillol had they met. Maillol was often seen
around Banyuls, sitting in front of plants or flowers and
sketching in one of his many small notebooks. The two artists also shared a preference for tranquility. As Mackintosh's
biographer, Robin Crichton, writes, "Mackintosh related to
forms and planes and structures but never much to people.

He was an outsider in daily life just as he was an outsider in his painting. He never integrated with the community." The reproductions of his paintings on display around Port-Vendres emphasize that aspect of his personality, as well as his background as an architect. They are very structured pieces, usually void of people, representing the pastel-colored homes along the water, the rock formations, and the ships in the bay.

In the fall of 1927, Mackintosh returned to London to be treated for tongue cancer, which he succumbed to a year later. To honor his last wish, it is believed that Margaret returned to their Catalan haven in May 1929 to scatter his ashes in the water at the entrance of the harbor.

Cerbère

The story of Paul Gauguin's visit to Cerbère in French Catalonia has often been left out of history books. A few art travel guides have even declared that Gauguin never set foot in the region. The omission has likely occurred because the story of the trip doesn't center on Gauguin as an artist, but more on Gauguin as a smuggler. A cryptic letter that Gauguin wrote from Cerbère to his friend the French Impressionist painter Camille Pissarro, dated August 13, 1883, made me curious to find out more. "I am at this moment very interested in Spain's affairs in which I am taking a somewhat active part," wrote Gauguin. "I will explain this to you later in secret."

In 1883, a former minister named Manuel Ruiz Zorrilla

gathered a group of armed revolutionaries to overthrow the newly restored monarchy in Spain and stage a return to a Republican government. Ruiz Zorrilla, who briefly served as Spain's prime minister in the early 1870s, now had aspirations to become president of the new government. He was plotting his way back from exile in France, where he had been living since 1875, when the First Spanish Republic had abruptly ended with King Alphonso II's ascension to the throne.

Portrayed as "a bit out of touch with the changes taking place in Spain," Ruiz Zorrilla was nevertheless backed by a few disgruntled soldiers who were not interested in serving the new monarchy. To build support, he joined forces with a secret organization called the Republican Military Association. They decided to raise arms on August 5, 1883. Gauguin's secret mission—put in place by Ruiz Zorrilla's right-hand man, A. Calzado—was to smuggle Zorrilla from the village of Cerbère, a few miles from the border, to the closest village in Spain, Port-Bou, less than four miles away. Ready to risk his life, or at least imprisonment, Gauguin planned to smuggle Ruiz Zorrilla under the nose of a border guard by hiding him in a bag of coal on a locomotive.

Gauguin eventually confided his extraordinary adventure to a few of his closest friends, including the painter George-Daniel de Monfreid, who later revealed in a letter, "Gauguin himself gave flight to his restless and fighting spirit by interesting himself in the Spanish revolutionary movement, led by Zorrilla… He told me then how he had come to our Roussillon…"

When the revolutionaries abruptly postponed the coup for

logistical reasons, the news did not travel quickly enough to all the soldiers stationed around Spain. The Spanish army, loyal to the monarchy, was able to foil the plot before it had even started. As one historian described, "In the days that followed, other military posts began to stir and a couple decided to take arms in solidarity. During the whole month of August, contradicting rumors circulated in regards to a *coup d'état* that finally never took place." The failed coup meant that Gauguin now had to conjure up a way to safely smuggle Ruiz Zorrilla back into French Catalonia to await his next window of opportunity. Like a true renegade, Gauguin boldly crossed the border with the Republican revolutionary hiding under bales of hay.

Why was Gauguin feeling so reckless that summer? This was a critical time for him. The devastating stock market crash of 1882 had left Gauguin unemployed. He had been a successful stockbroker for eleven years, providing for his wife, Mette Sophie Gad, and their four, soon to be five, young children. He considered himself a Sunday painter and occasionally participated in Impressionist exhibits under the guidance of Pissarro. Suddenly, he had the opportunity to pursue what he longed for, but to make such a decision would be drastic, to say the least. His difficult personality and lack of social grace would make it particularly challenging for him to find public support. But Gauguin believed in his talent. By the end of 1883, as his fifth child, Pola, was born, he committed to being an *artiste-peintre*. Hoping to lower his living costs, he had moved his family from Paris to the town of Orléans, where he had lived as a boy. Gauguin and Gad's marriage was already a stressful one, and the family's financial situation had become precarious.

Only one watercolor, signed "Cerbère, August 18, 1883. P.G.," survives from the time Gauguin spent stationed in Cerbère. In his journal *Avant et Après*, he recounted being accosted on the beach one morning by a police officer. "In Cerbère at the border, on the beach I draw," wrote Gauguin, "A gendarme from the Midi [*south France*], who suspects me of being a spy, says to me, who comes from Orléans.

— "Are you French?"
— "Why, certainly."
— "That's odd. *Vous n'avez pas l'accent (lakesent) français.* [You don't have a French accent.]"

Although the incident is difficult to translate without losing the play on pronunciation, the confrontation comes down to Gauguin feeling quite offended at being mistaken for a foreigner by a police officer who couldn't even pronounce the word *accent* properly.

Gauguin's "restless and fighting spirit," as described by de Monfreid, stemmed in part from his having been uprooted as a child and living his formative years in a foreign culture. When it came time to choose a career, the inevitable migratory instinct he had developed led him to join the merchant marine. He sailed twice to Brazil and once around the world. His restlessness stayed with him in his later years as he lived and worked in Panama, and then in the French colony of Martinique before his final sea voyage to Tahiti.

Paul Gauguin

Another contributing factor to Gauguin's willingness to get involved in Spain's affairs may have been the pride he felt in his Spanish ancestry. His great-grandmother had run off to Spain during the French Revolution, fallen in love, and married a Peruvian general. Their daughter, Gauguin's maternal grandmother, was the famous French feminist writer and adventurer Flora Tristán.

When Gauguin was two years old, his family moved to Peru for political and economic reasons. His father, a journalist and a Republican, did not support the election of Louis Napoleon Bonaparte, who was by then looking to dissolve the French National Assembly and claim himself Emperor. Tragically, Gauguin's father died at the young age of thirty-five during the long sea voyage. Under the strain of immeasurable grief and sudden financial uncertainty, Gauguin's mother, Aline, decided to move in with her relatives in Lima. She and her two young children stayed in the opulent home of her great-uncle, Pío de Tristán, who had been the last viceroy of Peru, ruling the territory from 1824 to 1826 in the name of King Fernando VII of Spain. Aline welcomed his kindness and generosity. For the next five years, Gauguin was exposed to the colorful and exotic city life of Lima. Gauguin heard stories about his courageous grandmother Flora, who had fought for the rights of the working class and for gender equality. Based in France, Flora had written several travel journals, including social commentaries on her time in Peru, and, later, on her life in England. Gauguin must have been inspired by Flora as he wrote his own travel journals from Tahiti years later, including the celebrated *Noa Noa*. As he tried to find his personal vision as a painter, he often thought of his formative years in Peru, his excursions across Latin America with the merchant marine, and his life-defining multicultural heritage. He once wrote to a friend, "You know that I have Indian blood, Inca blood in me, and it's reflected in everything I do. It's the basis of my personality; I try to confront rotten civilization with something more natural, based on savagery."

Although the paid smuggling mission for the Spanish revolutionaries surely held some romantic allure for Gauguin, his decision to undertake it was likely also driven by simple necessity. Gauguin was unemployed at the time and still had a family to support. As he wrote to his friend Pissarro, "If this revolution succeeds or stays active for a month, it could mean that in the near future, I will walk away with some money."

In the summer of 1884, Gauguin accepted 20,000 francs to travel south again and help Ruiz Zorrilla get across the border once more, but the plan was scrapped before he had the chance to enact it. This time Gauguin had been given orders to stay just north of Catalonia, in Montpellier. His plan had been to rent a boat and have it ready to navigate down the Mediterranean Sea, past the harbors of Collioure, Banyuls-sur-Mer, and Cerbère, and arrive in Spain. When Gauguin realized that the revolutionaries had abandoned their plans, the artist went sightseeing instead and visited the Fabre Museum. He made a sketch of Delacroix's *Aline, the Mulatto Woman*. Gauguin's biographer explained, "It was a portrait whose Arabic costume and setting were clearly destined to trigger something in a man whose disillusion with life in Europe was growing by the minute... [who] began to dream of more exotic settings for his own schemes."

When visitors come to Cerbère today, their adventures are noticeably more peaceful. They linger in the sun, walking past the rows of pastel-colored homes to the edge of the crystal-clear water, looking for the perfect picnic spot or swimming hole. The many coastal inlets hidden by large pine trees offer a small piece of heaven away from the crowds. The renowned Cerbère-Banyuls Natural Marine Reserve near Cap Peyrefite extends over 1,600 acres of sea floor, protecting the region's unique marine ecosystem and serving as a site for scientific research.

Some visitors discover Cerbère simply when they make a necessary train stop in the town and find their interest piqued by the viaduct with its enormous arches looming over the tracks. In the 1850s, the government agreed that a rail line to Spain was needed to boost commerce and tourism. The train station in Perpignan opened in 1858 and tracks were extended south, first to Port-Vendres in 1867, and then to Banyuls-sur-Mer in 1876. Almost all of Cerbère's 800 inhabitants during that period were connected in one way or another with the massive railway project. In 1878, the first train rolled in, passing along the majestic coastline and changing the town forever. From the time of de Monfreid's 1896 sightseeing trip through Catalonia with his friends Valtat and Maillol to Salvador Dalí's departure from Spain along with many other refugees at the onset of the country's 1936 civil war, passengers had to stop in Cerbère to clear customs. Passengers had to change trains at the station, since France and Spain used different rail gauges, a wartime strategy to prevent invasions that slowed down transportation for many years. The border station remains one of the main passage points between France and Spain, and for many years before tourism took center stage, its revenues sustained the town. The Cerbère train station continues to handle millions of tons of merchandise and assist thousands of passenger trains every year.

Years later, Gauguin reminisced about his stay in Catalonia. In August 1902 from Tahiti, as he suffered from many physical ailments, including an old ankle injury that was not healing well, he nostalgically confided in a letter to de Monfreid, "[I]t might be better for me to return for a change of climate. Then I might settle myself near you in the South... until I am ready to go to Spain for new subjects." Tragically, Gauguin never saw the Mediterranean coastline again. He passed away a year later on the remote island of Hiva Oa in French Polynesia.

CHAPTER 3

The Cult of Friendship

*Gatherings at George-Daniel de Monfreid's estate in **Corneilla-de-Conflent** at the foot of the Canigou Mountain—The spirit of Paul Gauguin reigns—A visit with Henri Matisse, Terrus, and Bausil—Exploring the region with Gauguin's widow, Mette Sophie Gad—De Monfreid and Gauguin's oldest son, Jean René, climb the Canigou.*

Le Domaine de Saint-Clément in Corneilla-de-Conflent

Corneilla-de-Conflent

"At 10:50 a.m., I head over with my bicycle to wait for Terrus and Matisse who arrive by train. We return on foot," wrote the painter George-Daniel de Monfreid on June 12, 1905, in his still-unpublished personal journal. This simple, matter-of-fact remark gave no indication of the extraordinary day that was about to unfold. De Monfreid, known for his hospitality and kindness, had invited a group of friends, including Terrus and Matisse from nearby Collioure, to lunch at his estate in Corneilla-de-Conflent, forty-six miles inland from the Côte Vermeille. He was eager to hear about Matisse's impressions of Catalonia and the effects it was having on his work. The two artists had last seen each other briefly in May at the sculptor Maillol's studio in Banyuls-sur-Mer.

Bicycle in hand, de Monfreid walked the two and a half miles back from the Villefranche-de-Conflent train station with Terrus and Matisse. As they approached one of the many arched passageways carved in the medieval ramparts, they looked up to admire the massive seventeenth-century Château Fort Libéria, ensconced high in the cliffs that surround the center of town. The fort, with its excellent artillery position, was built by Vauban and served the French army for over 350 years until it was abandoned in 1925. The fort dominates the town and steep hillside. Today, visitors can climb its impressive 734 steps to reach breathtaking views.

Villefranche-de-Conflent, now a UNESCO World Heritage site, sits at the strategic location where the Têt, Cady, and Rotja Rivers meet. As a result, it has been heavily fortified for centuries, and the town is seemingly impenetrable. The confluence of the three rivers nourishes the delicate apple and pear orchards of the region. It also provides water for the vast pastures of grass used for sheep farming.

As the three artists approached the village of Corneilla-de-Conflent, listening to the tinkling of bells from the animals grazing in the Cady Valley below, the majestic Canigou Mountain revealed itself on the horizon. At over 9,000 feet, the snowcapped Canigou has been revered by French and Spanish Catalans both past and present. The mountain overlooks rows of Corneilla's simple stone homes and the town's central square, where villagers congregate for the day's news. The distinct twelfth-century church of Saint Mary attracts visitors looking for remnants of Romanesque art, with its tall square tower and intricately carved doorway made of pink marble from the nearby Conflent quarry.

The Canigou is a symbol of unity for Catalans. Every June, to celebrate Saint John, or *la fête de Saint Jean*, a group of French Catalans carry a torch from Perpignan, the capital of French Catalonia, to the top of the mountain, where a metal cross decorated with the red and yellow Catalan flag stands. The torch is passed off to eagerly waiting Spanish Catalans, who then take it down the other side of the mountain. To promote their cultural and linguistic heritage, Catalans gather in towns and villages to dance the *sardana*, eat, and drink together. Bonfires are lit throughout the region. At dawn, many villagers collect flowers at the foot of the Canigou. They use medicinal herbs like St. John's wort and vervain to make small crosses to hang on the doors of their homes to bring health, protection, and a good harvest for the year. To reclaim the mountain's old charm, nearby communities have recently brought in five hundred donkeys, "*les ânes Catalans*," to counteract the presence of the 4×4 ATVs that have taken over the landscape.

Entering Corneilla-de-Conflent, de Monfreid, Matisse, and Terrus traveled down a gravel path past chestnut trees to a tall iron gate at the entrance de Monfreid's estate. The host invited Matisse and Terrus to take a seat at the long wooden table set up on the terrace shaded with large parasols. The view was spectacular. The cherry, kaki, and pear trees lined up the path to the garden that disappeared into the forest with the Canigou rising in the distance. The bright red roses by the terrace had burst into bloom. De Monfreid's son, Henry, who became a celebrated writer, said at the end of his legendary traveling days, "I always believed that the important and meaningful changes in our lives happened during chance encounters. Maybe that's what 'fate' is." Indeed, it was a chance encounter for Matisse, who had been on the verge of giving up painting as he ventured to Catalonia, to now find himself in the presence of de Monfreid and Terrus, two fiercely independent artists who would change his life and artistic direction forever. Their names may have been brushed aside, but when their stories are told, no one can dispute their significance in the development of modern art.

On the terrace of the Saint Clément castle, the three painters waited for the other guests, who had gone on a car expedition up the foothills of the Canigou for an awe-inspiring view of its peak. "Only around 1 o'clock do they arrive having had an excellent trip," wrote de Monfreid. The eclectic group included the Catalan painter Louis Bausil, Fernand Dumas, the Perpignan banker and patron of the arts who had been supporting many up-and-coming Catalan artists, his wife, Thérèse, and a local dentist, Amédée Calmel, who was the first to own Paul Gauguin's *Te reriora* (The dream). As they sat down for lunch, the conversation around the table turned to the topic that united them all—the art they had seen at the previous Salon des Indépendants in early spring in Paris, where Terrus and Matisse had exhibited paintings. The Salon had been created by a group of artists as a protest to the juried—and therefore more selective—Salon d'Automne. It was there that Matisse had sold his large Pointillist painting *Luxe, calme, et volupté*. Paul Signac had purchased it to hang in his dining room in Saint Tropez, next to Louis Valtat's *Femmes au bord de la mer* and Henri-Edmond Cross's *L'Air du soir*. Matisse had been encouraged by the sale, although he was now looking to break free from Pointillism.

De Monfreid shared details on the first retrospective of Paul Gauguin's work, which had taken place in Weimar, Germany, a few months earlier. The exhibit had included over thirty paintings on loan from de Monfreid and his friend

Gustave Fayet, who was a brilliant art collector from nearby Béziers. De Monfreid also revealed that he was in possession of Gauguin's paint box, untouched since its discovery in Gauguin's hut in Hiva Oa in French Polynesia after his death. De Monfreid explained to his guests that the French writer and navy doctor Victor Ségalen had brought it back after a trip to retrieve Gauguin's belongings. He had given it to de Monfreid earlier that spring in Paris, telling him that he was "the only one who deserved to hold on to it."

But the real treasure was being guarded not in Paris, but inside the castle of Saint Clément. De Monfreid invited his guests to join him in the living room. There, he showed them the mysterious wood carvings done by Gauguin in Tahiti, which had only been shown to a handful of visitors. In October 1900, Gauguin had written a letter to de Monfreid to let him know that he had shipped several works, not to Paris but directly to Villefranche-de-Conflent. On March 22, 1901, after sending his assistant to pick up the shipment at the train station, de Monfreid finally opened the crate to find several paintings and wood carvings, including *L'Idole à la coquille*, *L'Idole à la perle*, *Christ en croix*, *Hina*, *La stèle au Christ*, and *Quand le conteur parle*. In his letter, Gauguin noted, "[I]t would give me great pleasure if you would accept (not as a present, but as a proof of my friendship) all the woodcarvings from Tahiti." De Monfreid's second wife, Annette Belfis, was already the owner of the 1896 mask *Tehura*, which Gauguin had offered to thank her for posing for him in Paris. The originality and bluntness of Gauguin's woodcarvings, the blend of strikingly different cultural references, and

Gauguin's resonant call to "dare everything" left Matisse in shock.

In front of these primitive wood carvings and woodcuts from Tahiti, Matisse sensed a powerful shift in his artistic development. He was convinced that Catalonia had reunited an important group of forward-thinking artists who could help him find a new way to paint raw emotions through more expressive means, through color, like the violent *tramontana* wind that clears the sky to reveal breathtaking sunsets. He wrote, "I wanted to burn down the Ecole des Beaux-Arts with my cobalts and vermilions. I wanted to express my feelings without troubling what painting was like before me...Life and me, me and life—that's all that matters." It was clear that day that Gauguin's most passionate supporters lived in Catalonia and not in Paris.

Matisse's fascination with Gauguin had been growing. In 1899, although his family was struggling financially, he had been unable to resist buying one of Gauguin's first Tahitian paintings, *Le jeune homme a la fleur de tiaré*, which he kept for many years. In February 1905, he had viewed Fayet's extraordinary avant-garde collection at his private hotel in Paris. According to Fayet's descendants, close to 100 Gauguin paintings and carvings eventually went through his collection—a feat never to be repeated by either an individual or an art institution.

Instigated by de Monfreid, Fayet had purchased his first Gauguin paintings—*Les seins aux fleurs rouges* and *Les trois Tahitiens*—in 1900 for the price of 1,200 francs. De Monfreid had immediately shared his excitement in a letter to

Gauguin: "Your two paintings, which he appreciates for their artistic value, stand out exceedingly well in his collection, between a magnificent Cézanne and a Degas. He informs me that they dominate everything in their vicinity. Fayet will certainly do much for your reputation, not only in Béziers, but in Paris as well." Indeed, for the next few years, Fayet became Gauguin's *mécène*, determined to alleviate the artist's financial worries and let him focus on his work.

During Matisse's visit, Fayet also spoke highly of Gauguin's sculptures, as he let him study the Tahitian ceramic figure *Oviri*, which had caused a furor and been thrown out of the Salon de la Société Nationale des Beaux-Arts in 1895. *Oviri*, "the monstrous standing woman...towering above the body of a dead she-wolf," was considered too exotic, too savage, and its interpretation too ambigious. In a letter to his friend the painter Odilon Redon, Gauguin had simply stated that *Oviri* represented, "[n]ot death in life, but life in death." Today, a bronze casting stands on Gauguin's tomb in French Polynesia at the request of the artist.

Although the critics and most of the general public were still largely repulsed by his revolutionary artwork, Gauguin kept pushing his fellow artists to study primitive cultures, to return to the source, to help them create a new art, "with simple lines, dark contours, and the revolution of pure colors to portray the emotions of the artist instead of the actual landscape." Gauguin famously declared, "The Impressionists studied color, and color alone, as a decorative effect, but they did so without freedom, remaining bound by the shackles of verisimilitude...They focused their efforts around the eye, not in the mysterious center of thought." This message was applied early on by Matisse and our group of artists in Catalonia as they interpreted the landscape around them through their emotions, adding decorative or expressive elements to their paintings.

Matisse described this critical summer in his life to his biographer, who wrote, "It was only during his stay in Collioure that Matisse became fully aware of the powerful influence brought on by Gauguin, during a time of terrible upheaval." This momentous revelation would not have happened without de Monfreid, Gauguin's most devoted friend and confidant. The extraordinary treasures he held in Corneilla-de-Conflent would not be shown to the public in Paris until the Salon d'Automne of 1906, where the young Pablo Picasso would have his own epiphany.

Whether it was the excitement of discovering Gauguin's raw wood carvings at Saint Clément that fateful day in June 1905, or simply the hardy *rancio* wine that de Monfreid had been serving freely all afternoon, Matisse, with his cheeks flushed, could not return to Collioure that evening. As de Monfreid wrote in his journal, "Matisse is tipsy... Everyone decides to stay and spend the night: the house is full of make-shift beds." Early the next morning, the guests slipped out of Saint Clément quietly. "At four o'clock, I heard Matisse, Terrus, and Calmel leaving for the five o'clock train," wrote the humble host.

Who *was* George-Daniel de Monfreid, besides Gauguin's most trusted confidant? How did Catalonia become his adopted homeland? And why does he resemble King Leopold II

Baptism of Agnès de Monfreid, June 11, 1899,
Corneilla-de-Conflent. From the left, Louis Valtat and his wife,
Suzanne; George-Daniel de Monfreid behind his wife,
Annette Belfis; Clotilde and Aristide Maillol
(From the archives of the Friends of Louis Valtat Association)

of Belgium? The family history reads like a mystery novel. Some historians place his birth in New York, others in Paris. His mother, Marguerite Barrière, was a singer who loved the stage and toured throughout France. Sometime around 1854, while giving a concert in Aix-les-Bains, Marguerite met Gideon F.T. Reed, a wealthy jewelry businessman from Boston. Mr. Reed was in charge of international trade at the Reed and Tiffany Company—now the world-famous Tiffany—and traveled in style, often aboard his personal train, conducting business with royal family members across Europe. Short, overweight, and extremely generous, Mr. Reed lavished

Marguerite with expensive jewels, invitations to sumptuous dinners, and the latest fashion for attending magnificent balls with the *haute bourgeoisie*.

His kindness and connections made it easy for Marguerite to say *yes* when he asked her to return to the United States with him. To boost her social status, Marguerite boldly created a new name for herself and became Caroline de Monfreid (a variation of her mother's maiden name). But the trip was short-lived. Caroline returned to France to attend her father's funeral without her lover, but not without his funds. Having abandoned her career as a singer, she instead spent her time at the popular health resorts of Vernet-les-Bains and the hotel Sacaron de Luchon, also a favorite destination of the young and ravenous Leopold II of Belgium. The two became lovers and traveled together. It is rumored that they were even guests at the Russian court.

On March 14, 1856, Caroline gave birth to a son, whom she named George de Monfreid. But who was the father? According to de Monfreid's granddaughters, Gisèle and Amélie, he did not share any physical resemblance to Mr. Reed, and both believe that de Monfreid's biological father was King Leopold II. The social complications were significant, to say the least. Mr. Reed was married and had a family in the United States. Caroline was technically married as well, to a man named François Jacoby, who was exiled in Venezuela at the time. According to the family, Jacoby had been accused of stealing jewels that Caroline had received from Mr. Reed, and the wealthy businessman forced Jacoby to either leave the country or face the courts.

But the young George de Monfreid needed a birth certificate and papers to attend French schools. With his incredible connections at the U.S. consulate, Mr. Reed eventually obtained a certificate declaring that de Monfreid had been born in New York, to a fictitious father named Charles de Monfreid, a sailor lost at sea. "Uncle Reed," as de Monfreid called him, continued to care for Caroline and her young son. Although she was based in Paris, Caroline had fallen in love with Catalonia during her trips to Vernet-les-Bains and decided to search for a summer house nearby. In the spring of 1863, after a successful real estate negotiation from Mr. Reed, Caroline moved into Saint Clément with her seven-year-old son. A major renovation began, and the seventeenth-century farmhouse was expanded into the small castle that it is today.

De Monfreid eventually became a well-respected artist in his own right, choosing the name Daniel to sign his work. He painted primarily intimate portraits of family and friends, still lifes of flower bouquets and fruits, and Catalan landscapes, from which he drew his greatest inspiration. "Be as it may, I am a *naturalist*, in life as in painting," wrote de Monfreid, "but never a *realist*."

The artist spent long hours in his studio located in one of the towers of Saint Clément. Decorated with wooden benches covered in blue and red Persian throws, his *atelier* was flooded with natural light, offering solemn views of the Canigou and, at its base, the church tower and the red-tiled roofs of Corneilla-de-Conflent's narrow homes. As Gauguin once expressed to his friend, "Quite aside from your noble character, which always makes you dear to people who are worth anything, you are talented." From 1891, de Monfreid was a regular contributor to the Salon des Indépendants, and he eventually presented several well-received landscapes and portraits at the more distinguished Salon d'Automne.

However, the artist preferred to give his paintings away to friends and relatives rather than follow the traditional route of showing his work to attract gallery owners and potential dealers. Many of his paintings now hang in the Musée d'Orsay and the Musée d'Art Moderne in Paris, as well as museums in the south of France. The French painter Edgar Degas, who was enjoying wild success in France at the time, had admired de Monfreid's portraits in his Paris studio. De Monfreid boasted of the afternoon to his friend Bausil, "The old man Degas—the most spiritual but meanest man in Paris—came to see my paintings and complimented me. He looked over your portrait carefully and gave me nothing but praise!"

De Monfreid is particularly remembered for his generosity toward his friends. In the 1880s, he offered his close friend Maillol a bed and a warm meal at Saint Clément on particularly difficult days. In his journal entry on May 4, 1897, he wrote "I am going to pick up the Maillols to invite them as they are penniless." Maillol and his wife, by then the parents of a one-year-old boy named Lucien, stayed at Saint Clément until they received much-needed funds from the sale of one of Maillol's early sculptures. Their financial situation was sometimes so difficult that de Monfreid had to take care of Maillol's mail when he could not afford stamps.

None of his friends, however, depended on de Monfreid as much as Gauguin. The two artists had met in November 1887, upon Gauguin's return from a trip to Martinique and the Panama Canal. De Monfreid immediately took to Gauguin's work. As he explained, "I understood what Gauguin was looking for and, at the same time, I sensed that everything I had been taught about art was false." After his departure to the South Seas, when letters from his wife and friends became sparse, Gauguin could always count on de Monfreid's monthly mail and his willingness to accept every demand that he made. De Monfreid sent him everything from flower seeds and new shoelaces to prime canvas and paints. He sent money from the occasional sales of Gauguin's paintings whenever he could. These sales were often personally organized by de Monfreid, along with Vollard's help in Paris. Before presenting paintings to potential buyers, de Monfreid painstakingly repaired, waxed, and framed the canvases that arrived in poor shape from Tahiti, after taking care of the duty tax when the shipments arrived in either Paris or Villefranche-de-Conflent.

In 1893, when Gauguin returned to France—only to leave again permanently two years later—he arrived at the port of Marseilles desperate and lost with only four francs in his pocket. Fortunately, de Monfreid had made sure that there was money waiting for him at the local post office, enabling Gauguin to take the train back to Paris straight to de Monfreid's studio. A few years later, when Gauguin shipped the large wood panels *Guerre et paix* that Fayet had commissioned, de Monfreid generously delivered the wood carvings to Fayet, about ninety miles away in Béziers. The transaction was not easy for de Monfreid, as he recalled in a letter to Gauguin, "Fayet found your wood carvings beautiful, but...

It's always the same thing: he is reluctant about the price...I feared that he would turn us down...I then hurried the deal and told him he could keep the wood panels for 1500 francs. That's the best I could do! And believe me, I had to employ all the persuasion and diplomacy that I had." Gauguin, who was again desperately low on funds, was grateful for de Monfreid's efforts.

De Monfreid provided constant support and counsel without judgment, notably during Gauguin's fights with syphilis, influenza, and severe eczema contracted from a foot injury. In 1897, when Gauguin attempted to commit suicide by drinking arsenic, the first person he confided in was de Monfreid. "I went into the mountains," he wrote, "where my body would have been devoured by the ants...Whether the dose was too strong, or whether the vomiting counteracted the action of the poison, I don't know; but after a night of terrible suffering I returned home." Soon after, Gauguin revealed, "Before I died I wished to paint a large canvas," and sent de Monfreid a drawing of his masterpiece *D'où venons nous? Que sommes nous? Où allons nous?*, which he had started feverishly after his suicide attempt. It is impossible not to come slightly undone at the radiant beauty of the painting, which now hangs at the Museum of Fine Arts in Boston, when you understand the emotional abyss the artist had just overcome.

In August 1902, Gauguin considered returning to Europe to settle near de Monfreid in Catalonia and taking trips to nearby Spain for inspiration. De Monfreid advised him against the move, prophetically stating, "Now you are that legendary artist, who, from out of the depths of Polynesia, sends forth his disconcerting and inimitable work...Your enemies (and you have many as have all who trouble the mediocre) are now silent, do not dare to combat you, do not even think of it: for you are so far away! You must not return. Now you are as are the great dead. You have passed into the history of art." Gauguin decided to move to Atuona, Hiva Oa instead, hoping to find a "new and more savage subject matter." It was there that he died of a heart attack on May 8, 1903, at the age of fifty-five.

The Romanesque church of Saint Pierre in Corneilla-de-Conflent

When the news of Gauguin's death reached de Monfreid in France on August 23, 1903—almost four months later—he immediately called Fayet, who had become a strong supporter of Gauguin. De Monfreid quickly wrote a series of articles in different French papers and magazines to counteract the attacks that emerged, including the fabrication that Gauguin had died of leprosy. In these widely read publications, de Monfreid declared Gauguin to be the leader in modern art.

After Matisse's visit in the summer of 1905, de Monfreid opened his majestic home to another special guest: Gauguin's widow, Mette Sophie. She arrived on July 30 and spent the next three weeks visiting the Mediterranean coast with Dumas and Bausil, who proudly showed Madame Gauguin the beauty of Catalonia. Mette was happy to leave the harsh northern climate to enjoy what she called the sun-drenched "paradise of Saint Clément." At fifty-four, having never officially divorced Gauguin, Mette hoped the trip would finalize the details of Gauguin's succession rights and guarantee that her family would not be forgotten. In 1904, de Monfreid had received power of attorney over Gauguin's will. Mette also wanted to see Gauguin's work from Tahiti, much of which was still unknown to her. Since separating from Gauguin and moving back to Copenhagen, Mette had successfully provided for her family, mostly by teaching French and translating classic French novels into Danish, but also by occasionally selling a few of Gauguin's paintings.

De Monfreid enjoyed getting to know Mette, a tall

Scandinavian woman who wore her hair short and liked to join the men for a good cigar after dinner. Madame Gauguin appreciated the hospitality and warmth of de Monfreid and his wife, Annette, as well as the energy of their six-year-old daughter, Agnès de Monfreid, who ran freely around the property.

Mette's son Jean René was also lured by the mysterious man in Catalonia who had devoted his life to promoting his father's artistic career. Jean René, then twenty-eight, stayed in Corneilla-de-Conflent from early August through the end of October 1909. De Monfreid, who was known for being an avid cyclist, did not hesitate to introduce Jean René to long excursions around the countryside, "where the green seems exaggerated." De Monfreid often biked to Prades, Banyuls, Elne, or Perpignan to visit with friends, and sometimes traveled as far as Figueres or Gerona in Spanish Catalonia. One September afternoon, "I suggest a bicycle ride to the Canigou," wrote de Monfreid. Jean René Gauguin accepted the challenge and the two headed up the foothill to finally reach the forest road that led them to the Castell. From the popular view point, they looked up to admire the peak of the Canigou before heading back down. "At 5:30 we climb down the left bank of Saint Vincent [River]," noted de Monfreid. "Night is approaching and we race to the bottom. At 6:45 we are at the foot of the mountain, and at 7 in Vernet in complete darkness, at 7:45 at the house relatively tired." Luckily, there were therapeutic baths in Vernet to alleviate any suffering the next day. But as de Monfreid remembered, Jean René also took on less rigorous activities during his stay, and enjoyed his evenings "going to Corneilla to dance with the maids."

Unfortunately, the relationship between the Gauguins and de Monfreid deteriorated after their visits to Saint Clément, due to their differing perspectives on the preservation of Paul Gauguin's legacy. During his stay in Tahiti, Gauguin had compiled a unique manuscript entitled *Noa Noa*, which included observations, watercolors, photographs, and drawings. Upon Gauguin's death, Mette and her sons, who were hoping to make a large profit from it, encouraged the interest of several buyers. However, such a sale would guarantee that the manuscript would not stay in France. De Monfreid was firmly against the idea. After Gauguin's son Pola made an unexpected visit to de Monfreid's Paris studio and demanded the manuscript, de Monfreid took to his journal and wrote, "I tell him that I will hold firm until the end whatever lawsuit he wants to bring against me." Mette Gauguin and her sons, Jean René and Pola, never forgave him for interfering. Jean René's anger toward his father for abandoning his family inevitably transferred to the man who helped protect and insure Paul Gauguin's legacy. In later years he coldly referred to de Monfreid as "that swindler!" As for the original copy of *Noa Noa,* the Gauguin family did not sell it, and de Monfreid donated the manuscript to the Louvre in 1926.

George-Daniel de Monfreid's career has often been overshadowed by that of his son, Henry, who became one of France's greatest twentieth-century explorers and a celebrated travel writer. Growing up, Henry spent many carefree summers in Corneilla-de-Conflent with his mother, de Monfreid's first wife, Amélie Bertrand. "Saint Clément with its turrets, its iron gate…and these mountains surrounding it…all this made for an enchanted palace," remembered Henry in his autobiography.

In September 1910, at the age of thirty, Henry de Monfreid returned to Saint Clément, but this time he was fighting for his life, desperately sick with Malta fever he had contracted from drinking contaminated goat milk. Also known as brucellosis, the illness was responsible for many deaths in the early 1900s. Surrounded by doctors summoned from Prades and Montpellier, Henry suffered for months with fever, painful stomach and kidney aches, and debilitating headaches. "I'm very worried for Henry," wrote his father during one of many sleepless nights. "The fever is here, relentless!…He suffers from excruciating pain…We are desperate."

A young art student, Armgart Freudenfeld, who was visiting Saint Clément at the time, agreed to help nurse Henry back to health. More importantly, she agreed to take care of Henry's two small boys, Lucien and Marcel, after the sudden departure of their mother.

In between fevers, the future writer realized that he had to make bold choices in order to make his life count. He was tired of the unfulfilling jobs he had been pursuing as a door-to-door coffee salesman, a mechanic, a chauffeur, and milk producer, among others. The near-death experience that lasted eight months propelled him to see the world. As he reflected later in life, "Of all the insanities that we find in humanity, it is that man, during his time on earth, where he lives only once, does not have the curiosity to explore it completely." Considering the worldwide adventures his grandchildren and great-grandchildren have undertaken since, leading them to locations such as Vietnam, Cambodia, Nigeria, the South Pacific, the United States, and Reunion Island, it seems Henry de Monfreid's message has become the family's mantra.

When he left Corneilla-de-Conflent, Henry de Monfreid decided to pursue his passion for the sea, which had begun in 1885 when his father took him on his first long-distance nautical trip to Algiers when Henry was just six years old. He set sail for Djibouti, Ethiopia, and decided to build a family with Armgart, who gave birth to three children, Gisèle, Amélie, and Daniel. Throughout his time in Africa, Henry traveled to Somalia, Kenya, and along the Red Sea, trading everything from coffee and leather to the more lucrative hashish and arms. Like Gauguin, Henry de Monfreid preferred to live with the locals, learning their customs, way of life, and language. His attitude, as his biographer George Paré observed, was that "the only viable role is as visitor to this reality, to be a tourist of one's life, always curious, in motion, surprised, searching to understand it, and sometimes also, maybe a bit too often, forgetting it." I would venture that the last comment was directed at his paternal duties toward his children, who had to endure the consequences of his pirate ways, which incurred the occasional incarceration. When his first book, *The Secrets of the Red Sea*, was published in 1931, when Henry was fifty-two, it was an immediate success and propelled him to international fame. He wrote an additional seventy books before he passed away on December 13, 1974.

*   *   *

Henry de Monfreid had been in Africa when he received the news that his father had passed away at the age of seventy-three after falling from a ladder as he picked kaki fruits from a tree in front of the terrace of Saint Clément. His body rests in the family's mausoleum in the town's cemetery, a few steps away from the church of Saint Mary. Henry's stepsister, Agnès, inherited the estate and continued to invite artists to enjoy its idyllic location in the quiet village of Corneilla. In the 1950s, during the annual Casals Music Festival in nearby Prades, Agnès welcomed musicians who had traveled from around the world to play alongside the Catalan cellist and conductor Pau Casals. One particular musician, the Polish-American pianist Mieczyslaw Horszowski, developed close ties with the de Monfreid family and became a regular guest, visiting every year. In 1960, he also spent a lengthy convalescence at Saint Clément, recuperating in the "enchanted palace."

The tradition had been passed on. Sharing their table with musicians, sculptors, painters, and writers, some legendary, some simply passionate, the owners of the castle of Saint Clément always generously fostered the arts, and the majestic surroundings of Corneilla-de-Conflent continued to instill artists with renewed energy and creativity.

CHAPTER 4

The Mecca of Creativity

*The Spanish Catalan sculptor Manolo Hugué makes a home in **Céret**, French Catalonia—The cherry blossoms and sunshine attract painters Juan Gris, Chaim Soutine, Moise Kisling, and Marc Chagall—The composer Déodat de Séverac discovers the Catalan Cobla musicians—Evenings at the Grand Café with "la bande à Picasso"—Picasso and Georges Braque rent the Delcros home and develop Cubism—Gatherings at Frank Burty Haviland's monastery, Les Capucins—Salvador Dalí's grand entrance at the bullfighting arena in 1965.*

Fernande Olivier and Pablo Picasso, 1904
(Réunion des Musées Nationaux / Art Resource, NY)

Céret

In the winter of 1909, when their lives in Paris had become bleak and expensive, the Spanish Catalan sculptor Manuel Martínez i Hugué, known as Manolo, and his friend, the American painter Frank Burty Haviland, ventured south toward the sun and tranquility of the French countryside. The two artists first stopped in Banuyls-sur-Mer to visit with Maillol, who invited them to stay. But when the vicious *tramontana* wind picked up, Manolo and Haviland continued on their trek to Vernet-les-Bains, which was famous for its healing hot water springs. Unconvinced, however, that they should share the streets with ghastly tuberculosis patients looking for their next spittoon, Haviland tossed a coin, as the legend goes, to help them pick their next destination. Fate led them to Céret, a small village in the heart of the Vallespir region, sheltered by the eastern side of the Pyrenees.

When they arrived at the Hôtel du Canigou, on Rue Saint Ferréol, Manolo and Haviland were greeted by the owner, Armand Janer, who offered them room and board for just three francs. The artists felt the city hardships melt away and decided to stay. They relayed the good news to their friends in Paris, many of whom would eventually make the trip themselves, trading depressing drizzle and dilapidated studios for warm sunshine and a room overlooking the prominent Canigou Mountain.

With its rich music scene and year-round festivals, its colorful markets and peaceful country setting, Céret offered authentic Catalan living, while keeping Manolo on the right side of the border. The sculptor, with his striking dark eyes, dark face, and dark hair, had deserted from mandatory service in the Spanish army and could not return home. Settling in Céret was the perfect compromise. Manolo and his wife, Jeanne Rochette, nicknamed "Totote," easily integrated into their new community, eventually making a home for themselves with their adopted daughter, Rose. The low cost of living in Céret meant a more carefree existence for Manolo, which suited the amicable artist, who was known for his occasional laziness. Although he would soon be recognized as one of the greatest Spanish sculptors of his generation, his day-to-day existence in the early 1900s depended mostly on the generosity of his friend Haviland and his Parisian art dealer, Daniel-Henry Kahnweiler, who in 1909 was beginning to sell the artist's work more regularly.

In one crafty letter, Manolo informed Kahnweiler that he was ready to create larger sculptures and that he needed more money to cover the expenses. Like a good mother hen, Kahnweiler obliged. Then "[o]ne day I got a letter," divulged the art dealer, "saying, 'I have just sent you a large sculpture. It is a kneeling woman who, if she stood up, would be five feet tall.' In reality, of course, she was about fifteen inches high. Of course, if she had stood up..." Kahnweiler put his letter down and had a good laugh as he realized only the charming Manolo could get away with such a mischievous double cross.

Kahnweiler considered Manolo's sculptures to be "great art, fresh and close to the earth." The sculptor found his inspiration as he walked through the fields around Céret, meeting cattle farmers, grape pickers, and the peasants who harvested the rows and rows of cherry trees, which were bursting with sweetness and color. Manolo sketched Catalan workers for hours and later immortalized them in clay and bronze. He reflected, "It therefore all came, mostly, from my walks in the countryside."

In the early 1920s, as his reputation grew, the Catalan sculptor was chosen to construct a war memorial for the town of Arles-sur-Tech, which he worked on while his friend Maillol sculpted the war memorial for Céret. The close friends often celebrated Christmas in Céret together, breaking bread with their friends Gustave Violet and Étienne Terrus. As Manolo's biographer, Rafael Benet, wrote, "The Vallespir was like a motherland for Manolo—even if it was not his birthplace, he was reborn there."

The villagers of Céret befriended Manolo, who was fluent in Catalan, and they quickly warmed to his traveling companion, Haviland. The tall, lanky artist, who had a handsome face and black hair that he diligently parted in the middle, had chosen to become a painter even though his family, particularly his father, considered it "a lazy man's career." Having emigrated from the United States to Limoges, France, Frank's grandfather David Haviland built an extraordinary business in porcelain, which went on to provide adornment for the tables of European royal families and U.S. presidents.

Frank tried to join in the operations when his father Charles took over the successful Haviland Company, but his heart was not in it. He found the courage to pursue his own career, always remaining quite generous with his struggling artist friends. "I only really helped, supported Manolo, who moreover offered me drawings," insisted Haviland. "He was a good and happy companion."

The two friends were joined by the French composer Déodat de Séverac, who had originated the idea to move south, having himself been raised in Toulouse. Céret, where music emerged from every festival and religious procession celebrated by the villagers, represented divine intervention for Séverac. Céret had much to gain from Séverac as well, considering that he, along with the musicians Claude Debussy and Maurice Ravel, had been labeled "the trio of new French music."

The composer, who had a thick mustache and full black hair combed back, was moved by Céret's passion for music. The village was home to a musical association called l'Harmonie du Vallespir, as well as to three Cobla orchestras and an active church choir. Séverac's friend, the Catalan sculptor Violet, remembered their first Cobla concert: "One night in Céret, behind the stage, we listened, Déodat and I, to the *Cobla des Peps* of Figueres... Déodat's eyes were filled with tears and he was trembling." Once the music stopped, Séverac grabbed Violet by the arm and declared, "I absolutely must do something with this land here, with this music, with its values, its traditions, its light." In awe of the unique sounds that the Cobla instruments produced, Séverac feverishly incorporated them into the new three-act symphony piece, titled *Héliogabale*, that he had started upon his arrival in Céret. The composition was performed in Béziers for a crowd of 13,000 spectators, with over 400 musicians, 160 choir members, and sixty dancers. The lyrical tragedy was later received with critical acclaim in Paris.

The warm evenings of the Catalan countryside, protected by the Canigou, amplified Séverac's love of the open-air theater. He wrote, "The Catalan instruments...are perfect instruments for the outdoors, because they can be simultaneously cheerful, comical, dramatic, and expressive." In 1911, a month before Pablo Picasso arrived in Céret, Séverac put together a large production with musicians from across Catalonia to celebrate the fiftieth anniversary of Céret's music society. The arena welcomed thousands of enthusiastic spectators who came to listen to and applaud Séverac's folkloric piece

Le Pont du Diable—the Devil's Bridge—in Céret

El cant del Vallespir (The song of the Vallespir). The villagers were still humming the lyrics when Picasso and Georges Braque dropped their bags in town, forever altering the legacy of Céret.

Picasso first arrived in mid-July 1911 and rented a room at the Hôtel du Canigou. By then, his friend Haviland had moved out of the hotel and into the Maison Alcouffe on Avenue Francesc-Irla. The house, which still stands today, overlooks the magnificent Pont du Diable bridge. The bridge was built in 1341 and boasts an incredible 150-foot-long arch, which rises seventy-two feet over the Tech River at its highest point. Haviland agreed to let Picasso set up his studio in one of the rooms, accompanied by the pet monkey he brought with him from Paris. Haviland and Picasso shared a common interest in African art. Haviland's vast collection of primitive sculptures and masks captivated the Cubist master. Manolo, Picasso, and Haviland often gathered at the Maison Alcouffe, discussing their work, their theories, and their techniques. They might have shared a *suquet de peix*, a popular Catalan seafood stew with saffron, or had a glass of wine together as Totote sang and played nostalgic tunes on the guitar. Inspired by the company of his friends, Picasso wrote to his art dealer, Kahnweiler, that he was already hard at work, often late into the night, and had begun a painting titled *Poet and Peasant*.

The loud and spirited gatherings at the Grand Café, located on the corner of Boulevard Maréchal Joffre and Rue Saint Ferréol, were also in full swing. Picasso and Manolo, who both enjoyed playing practical jokes, surprised their table of friends one evening by wearing old black-and-gray derby hats that Braque had sent in the mail and completing the look with "false mustaches and sidewhiskers applied with cork." The scene, with a lively Séverac playing at the piano, must have given the villagers a taste of what was to come, now that the "Parisian" artists had overtaken their town.

Braque and his future wife, Marcelle Lapré, arrived in Céret on August 17th, two days after Picasso was reunited with his lover, Fernande Olivier. Braque was "a man of extraordinary elegance," recalled Kahnweiler. "[He] used to wear very simple blue suits with a special cut... [and] black, square-toed shoes. Like Max Jacob, he had a black string tie." Braque had also been wearing a Kronstadt, or "melon" hat, in honor of the painter Paul Cézanne.

It was Braque who had led the first official Cubist exhibition in Paris, organized by Kahnweiler in November 1908. As the story goes, Matisse, who was serving as a member of the jury of the Salon d'Automne that year, had opened a box of Braque's paintings—which were subsequently refused— and immediately wrote to the art critic Louis Vauxcelles, informing him that the French painter was now "making little cubes." Once Kahnweiler took possession of the rejected paintings, he decided to exhibit them himself. Vauxcelles examined each one carefully and announced in his widely read art review, *Gil Blas*, "[Braque] constructs deformed metallic men, terribly simplified... despises form, reduces everything, places and figures and houses, to geometrical schemes, to cubes." Giving a name to this style, just as he had done in 1905 with Fauvism, Vauxcelles declared that a new art movement called Cubism had been born.

Braque and Picasso—who, at the time, had never publicly exhibited his Cubist paintings—are recognized by most art historians as "[t]he first and greatest Cubists." At the onset of the Cubist movement, the two artists took the lead from French painter Paul Cézanne and decomposed objects in their paintings into geometrical shapes: cubes, cylinders, and triangles. They subsequently exposed objects in a new way, showing all sides—front, back, top, and bottom—all at once. This effect caused an uproar among both the general public and the critics, who found the paintings confusing and radical.

By the time Braque and Picasso met in Céret, they were shifting from Analytic Cubism to Synthetic Cubism, turning their artwork into mesmerizing kaleidoscopes and using mostly brown and gray paint. Braque and Picasso reduced chosen objects, such as mountains, rooftops, musical instruments, wineglasses, and bottles, down to simple fragments that were almost unrecognizable. The objects seemed to have been flattened onto the canvas. Although some of these paintings can be difficult to decipher, Braque reminded the viewing public that it was all the same to him "whether a form represents a different thing to different people or many things at the same time." Some of his forms, according to Braque himself, "have no literal meaning whatsoever." The two artists typically preferred not to comment on their paintings from Céret, and instead let their work speak for itself, which might explain all the contradicting "official" interpretations.

While in Céret, Picasso rented the second floor of the Maison Delcros on Rue des Evadés. There, Braque set up his studio as well in a bright room with a high ceiling and French doors opening out onto a large stone balcony. The expansive home, which is now a private residence, is surrounded by a beautiful garden with an unobstructed view of the Albères mountain range. Picasso felt immediately energized in Braque's presence. "Braque is here," he informed Kahnweiler, "I would need 1,000 francs to stay here as long as I'd like to stay, to do what I want to do. I think that Braque is very happy to be here. I've already shown him the whole area and he already has a lot of ideas in mind."

During the three weeks they spent together, the two artists pushed each other to see new perspectives, the way André Derain and Henri Matisse had done a few years earlier at the onset of Fauvism, seventeen miles away in Collioure. Braque once humbly described Cubism as a means "whose purpose was above all to put painting within the reach of my own gifts." Indeed, he did not draw as skillfully and effortlessly as Picasso did, but he compensated for that weakness by having, according to his art dealer, a "sensitivity to the subtleties of light and space," "ethical rigor rivaling Cézanne's," and the creative insight to introduce new revolutionary techniques, such as stenciled lettering and *papier collé*, which, in Céret, included applying clippings from the local newspaper, *L'Indépendant*, directly onto the canvas. Adding layers to the construction of Cubism, Braque also used a comb as a tool to make *faux-bois*, a trompe-l'oeil wood-graining technique he had learned during his earlier career as a housepainter.

Although Braque was brilliant in advancing Cubism with these innovative techniques, Picasso often embraced them so quickly and efficiently that history sometimes, unfortunately, dims the lights on their true inventor. It is fascinating to note how similar their paintings were during the time between the 1908 exhibition and the summer of 1911 in Céret, even when they were apart and working separately. The distinction is made even finer by the fact that Picasso and Braque often signed their paintings on the back in order not to "disturb the construction, the architecture of the painting, which they wanted to be so strong and solid."

The camaraderie between the two artists was undeniable. Picasso had nicknamed Braque "Wilbourg" after one of the Wright brothers, who made headlines in 1903 for their bold flight in a self-made airplane over the hills of Kitty Hawk, North Carolina. The pilots had then exhibited their skills in Le Mans, France, in 1908, thrilling thousands of spectators, many of whom had previously expressed doubt and denial. The artists could easily compare themselves to the two brothers as inventors, daring and confident in the face of criticism and skepticism. Picasso and Braque also loved the spirit of legendary Buffalo Bill. Their friend the American writer Gertrude Stein had introduced them to the adventure novels of the Far West. Picasso sometimes signed his letters with *Ton Pard* ("Your Pard"), taken from the cowboy's friendly term "partner."

The artists even sent messages back and forth to one another through their paintings. Take Picasso's *Guitare, feuille de musique et verre* with its partial newspaper clipping at the edge of the frame and its sly message: *La bataille est engagé* ("The battle is on"). Braque commented, "During [the Cubist] years, Picasso and I said things to one another that will never be said again...that no one will ever be able to understand...things that would be incomprehensible, but that gave us great joy...All that will end with us." According to William Rubin, the author of *Picasso and Braque: Pioneering Cubism*, during the four months after Picasso left Céret and Braque stayed behind, the two artists "produced some of their greatest Cubist paintings—the outcome of their cross-fertilization back in August" in French Catalonia.

Braque decided to stay in Céret through the fall, and did not leave until mid-January 1912. "[T]he season promises to be splendid!" he wrote to Kahnweiler, "What publicity! Every day I have to contend with the inhabitants of Céret who want to see some Cubism." In September, Braque made a trip to Collioure. "[I]t is very pretty," he wrote, "and if I had the time, I would like to do a few landscapes there. As soon as I arrived, I ran into Matisse, who showed me his latest canvases," including *Intérieur aux aubergines*. Braque returned to Céret, and, inspired by Matisse's *La fenêtre ouverte* overlooking the Taillefer and Sailfort peaks, immediately set up his easel in his studio to catch the frame of the window, the stone balcony, and the Boularic peak in the background in his own *La fenêtre à Céret*.

Throughout his stay in Catalonia, Braque counted on the financial support of his art dealer, who sent him money to cover his hotel bill, as well as two hundred francs a month for living expenses in exchange for paintings to sell in his Parisian gallery. Kahnweiler played a crucial role in keeping his painters fed and happy and able to focus on their work. As he noted, "[I]t wasn't simply about selling paintings; it was really about allowing painters to work free from financial anxiet- ies." Convinced that their paintings would one day "domi- nate the scene," Kahnweiler invested while the general public laughed on. Luckily, there was also a well-financed group of true avant-garde art collectors, including Stein in Paris and the Russian Sergei Shchukin whose collection is now on dis- play at the Pushkin Fine Arts Museum and the Hermitage in St. Petersburg.

When Picasso returned to Céret in the summer of 1912, he had a new lover with him, Eva Gouel, whose name at birth was Marcelle Humbert. He had left Paris abruptly, almost empty-handed, running away from his former lover, Fernande Olivier, who still hoped for reconciliation. Upon arriving in Céret, Picasso made Kahnweiler promise not to tell anyone his whereabouts and proclaimed, "Marcelle is very sweet. I love her very much and I will write this in my paintings." He immediately did so in *Violin: Jolie Eva*. Inspired once again by Céret, the artist noted, "I believe my painting has been gaining in robustness and clarity..."

Picasso could count on his Catalan friends to help him settle in. "Manolo has given me some paints," he informed Kahnweiler as he moved into the Maison Delcros, "but... I have no palette. Terrus has lent me an easel...In spite of everything, I'm working." As he toured the house, remember- ing the previous summer with Braque, Picasso was shocked to find his painting *Notre avenir est dans l'air,* which he thought had been lost, still hanging on the wall of his studio.

But Picasso lacked many items necessary to make the rooms feel like home, so he pleaded with Kahnweiler to send him "sheets, pillows, bolsters, blankets, my linen, and my yellow kimono with flowers. I'm not sure what you'll have to do to arrange all this, but I've more faith in you than in myself." He also asked for a wide variety of paint colors, a palette, his stencils, and metal combs to make *faux-bois*.

His creative energy was in full swing. Everything and everyone he encountered could spark a new idea in the prolific artist. One Sunday, as he and Eva listened to a man playing the bagpipes, Picasso envisioned attempting a copperplate etching of the musician, as he had seen in Gauguin's work. But still Picasso missed working with Braque: "What's happened to our walks," he wrote to his friend, "and our exchanges of feelings?" and, in another letter, "It's really too bad the phone in your place doesn't reach Céret. Such good conversations about art..."

His mind was also preoccupied by the rumor that Fernande Olivier was planning an unexpected trip to Céret. After asking Kahnweiler for a few thousand francs to cover expenses in case he and Eva had to leave town suddenly, Picasso did not hesitate to ask him to play intermediary in his personal life as well. "[I]f you should see Fernande, you can tell her that she can expect nothing from me, and I should be quite happy never to see her again," he instructed. When Fernande indeed arrived in Céret, accompanied by their friend Germaine Pitxot who had hosted the couple in Cadaqués during the summer of 1910, the situation proved too difficult for Picasso. He promptly left Céret, but with a heavy heart:

"I'm very bothered to have to leave this place; it's been good to be in a large house where I've had space, and I've liked the countryside."

In 1913, upon a third (and less dramatic) visit for Picasso, the villagers saw their town transform into a mecca of creativity with the arrival of several artists, including the poet Max Jacob, and the Cubist painters Juan Gris and Auguste Herbin, who completed over twenty paintings during his month-long stay. "La Bande à Picasso," as the group of friends was nicknamed, continued to meet in the evenings at the Grand Café. Seated at a table and spilling out onto the sidewalk, they discussed the day's work and shared news from Paris and Barcelona while smoking Gauloises cigarettes and drinking glasses of absinthe.

The group celebrated Haviland's recent purchase of Le Domaine des Capucins, an old convent that overlooks the village and has since been painted by most of the artists who have traveled to Céret. Haviland put down even deeper roots in January 1914, when he married Joséphine Laporta, a native of Céret, during a beautiful countryside ceremony. The event was attended by most of the villagers, who came to wish the couple a long and happy life together. Terrus, a guest at the wedding, related the news to Matisse back in Paris, as the Fauvist painter enjoyed receiving updates on the latest gatherings in French Catalonia.

La Bande à Picasso occasionally gathered in Céret's packed bullfighting arena to watch the matadors on hot summer afternoons. Picasso, Eva, and their guest, the poet Max Jacob, were captivated by bullfighting, and even traveled to Spanish

Catalonia for two days in August 1913 to watch an important bullfight in Figueres. Today, the arena in Céret no longer
welcomes matadors, as bullfighting was banned in July 2011.
On one side of the arena, near Rue de la Sardane, visitors can
admire the large wrought-iron monument entitled *Sardane de
la paix*, based on Picasso's well-known drawing *Danse de la
paix,* while on the other side, by Place de la Résistance, there
is a reproduction of *Toréro*, a sculpture by Manolo of a digni-
fied bullfighter.

For his inner circle of confidants, Picasso tended to favor
writers and poets over other painters. Jacob, who harbored a
quiet devotion to the painter, was one of his closest friends.
Picasso did not hesitate to pay for Jacob's trip to Céret, asking Kahnweiler, "Would you be kind enough to give him
the money for the trip and also some pocket money for his
expenses? Put it on my account." The poet, described by Kahnweiler as "one of the wittiest and most comical men in the
world" with "eyes of an extraordinary tenderness," described
a typical day at Picasso's home: "My day begins at six o'clock.
A prose poem gets me going. At eight, Mr. Picasso in a dark
blue or simple twill robe has just brought me a chocolate and a
heavy and tender croissant... The windows of my huge white
room would like to see the Canigou (alas, rain)... Each day I
learn to admire the greatness of spirit of Mr. Picasso, the true
originality of his tastes, the delicacy of his senses."

During the day, the shopkeepers might have seen Picasso,
Eva, and Jacob lingering in the square Les 9 Jets, shaded by
the large plane trees, after Picasso finished a quick sketch
of the famous fountain that has been running continuously

Le Grand Café in Céret

since 1913. Or they might have overheard a heated argument between Manolo and Gris, sitting at the Grand Café. "They were very good friends," insisted Kahnweiler, "but in regard to ideas, they didn't get along at all... Cubism has always been quite alien to [Manolo]... He always saw things with the good sense of the peasant." Like Manolo, Gris had skipped his military service and, therefore, could not return to Spain, but Céret offered the familiarity of his homeland.

Gris, who had been Picasso's neighbor in Paris, was happy to be working with the Cubist master again. The young painter stayed in Céret for four months, renting a home at the corner of Place du Barri and Rue Vell, next to the imposing Porte de la France, which is a fortified gateway that was part of the city's original rampart. Before his trip, Gris had exhibited his painting *Hommage à Picasso* in Paris, which sealed his reputation as a Cubist painter. Although Gris considered Picasso to be his teacher and mentor, Gertrude Stein acknowledged that Gris "was the one person that Picasso would have willingly wiped off the map"—a clear testament to Gris's talent. His biographer noted that in Céret, Gris "[c]ompleted some of the boldest and most mature statements of his cubist style, with landscape still lifes that compress interiors and exteriors into synthetic cubist compositions such as *Le Canigou*" and his series of clowns, including *Les deux pierrots*. His 1913 paintings *Paysage et maisons à Céret* and *Paysage à Céret* were striking in color, in contrast to the Cubist tendency toward monochromatic earth tones. They revealed the artist's close relationship with Matisse, the master of color, who would spend time again with Gris in Collioure as World War II began.

Juan Gris returned to Céret with his wife, Josette, in the winter of 1921. Remembered by his art dealer as "the purest man and the most faithful friend imaginable," Gris was by then suffering from severe asthma attacks which would eventually take his life at the young age of forty, though at the time his doctors had misdiagnosed him with tuberculosis.

When Gris and his wife were not resting, reading by the fireplace at the Hôtel Garretta on Rue Saint Ferréol, they could be found practicing their steps on the dance floor. "Gris loved to dance," remembered Kahnweiler, "and since he did everything very seriously, as we used to say, he used to buy those little booklets that were published in those days and teach himself the new dances, which at that time were the tango and dances of that kind." His lessons paid off, and "Don Juan Gris" and his wife proudly won the fox-trot contest in Céret during the New Year's celebrations that welcomed in 1922.

The young Surrealist painter André Masson also traveled south after World War I, although in his case he was looking for a place to heal from wounds sustained on the battlefield. He had first been drawn to Collioure, but eventually settled in Céret, on Rue de l'Hôpital. The artist was influenced by Picasso's Cubist work, but he soon joined the Surrealist movement, experimenting with pre–Jackson Pollock avant-garde techniques like "automatic writing" and throwing sand on glue-covered canvases. On February 13, 1920, inside Céret's St. Ferréol Hermitage church, Masson married his Catalan fiancée, Odette Caballé, and asked Manolo and Haviland to serve as his witnesses.

Living not far from Masson was the painter Chaïm Soutine from Belarus (part of Russia at the time), who rented a room in the Maison l'Evêque from 1919 to 1922. Soutine was not known for joining the festivities in Céret, and he did not leave a positive impression on the villagers. He often wandered the streets, drunk and unkempt, with his dirty blue worker's overalls covered with old paint stains, mumbling to himself and never acknowledging passersby. The artist did not speak French well, and his Catalan was even worse, which made it almost impossible to communicate with him. Nevertheless, he was not known for his gracious manners.

During his stay in Céret, Soutine was, however, extraordinarily productive, painting over 300 works of art. His art dealer, the gallery owner and Polish poet Leopold Zborowski, surprised him one day with a visit. Happening to come in at quite the opportune moment, Zborowski was able to save some 150 canvases, but the mad painter had already thrown more than 100 into the fireplace of the Hôtel Garetta. Most of the rescued paintings were bought by the famous art collector Dr. Albert Barnes and are now part of the Barnes Foundation near Philadelphia. Zborowski was amazed by Soutine's bizarre lifestyle. "Do you know how he paints?" he asked his friends. "He wanders about the countryside, where he lives like a poor wretch in a sort of pigsty. He gets up at three o'clock in the morning and, laden with his canvases and colors, walks a good twelve miles to find a spot that he likes. Then he walks back to his place of sleep, forgetting even to eat. He removes his canvas from the frame, though, and after laying it over the one he did the day before, lies down next to it and drops off to sleep." Remembered by his peers for his unique artistic achievements rather than his social skills, Soutine passed away in 1943, with Picasso present at his funeral.

Even so, Soutine did befriend other exiles in Paris, who shared similar stories of religious persecution in Tsarist

Russia, including Pinchus Kremegne and Marc Chagall. Kremegne had convinced Soutine to visit Ceret, after he himself had fallen in love with the village. Kremegne arrived in 1918 and eventually bought a home and installed a large studio where he lived and worked periodically until his death in 1981. In 1927, Chagall arrived in Céret with his wife, Bella, and their twelve-year-old daughter, Ida. The discreet family lived in Mas Lloret, a large cream-colored home with light blue shutters. Today, the house still stands at the edge of the Tech River, surrounded by fragrant bell-shaped mimosas. The property is on the outskirts of Céret, but Chagall treasured his daily walks to the village, whether it was to order paints and brushes at the store, or simply to pick up cherries on market day. "There, in the south," the artist observed, "for the first time in my life, I saw that rich greenness—the like of which I had never seen in my own country."

Before arriving in Céret, Chagall had been awarded the prestigious task of illustrating the seventeenth-century fables of Jean de la Fontaine. Vollard, an art collector turned editor, believed in Chagall's "supernatural" visions as a painter, even though the French National Assembly was vigorously protesting the decision to have a Russian artist provide the illustrations for the legendary French poet's work. As Vollard explained, "[I]t was precisely on account of the Oriental sources of the fabulist that I had pitched on an artist whose origins and culture had rendered him familiar with the magic East." In the end, Chagall contributed close to one hundred "dazzling gouaches," which were later transferred as etchings. "When I held a lithographic stone or a copper plate," Chagall later described, "it seemed to me that I was touching a talis-man. It seemed to me that I could put all my sorrows and my joys into them…everything that has crossed my life in the course of the years."

When the artist had to leave Céret, he surprised one store owner whom he had befriended by entrusting him with twenty-eight gouaches, which he picked up a few months later upon his return for a second stay. As this remarkable gesture demonstrates, many of the artists who journeyed to Céret had developed a deep kinship with the villagers. They had come for inspiration and tranquility, but had also been welcomed by the Catalan spirit of generosity, trust, and loyalty.

This spirit of friendship was never more apparent than on March 24, 1921, the day the composer Déodat de Séverac passed away in Céret. The villagers mourned the beloved composer, their adopted son who had elevated Catalan cul-ture through his musical legacy. In the weeks prior to Séverac's death, de Monfreid, then sixty-five years old, did not hesi-tate to climb on his bike and pedal the twenty miles from his home in Corneilla-de-Conflent to Céret, to spend time with his ill friend. On the fateful day of March 24, after receiving a telegram from Violet stating that Séverac's condition had worsened, de Monfreid made the trip once more. The painter jumped on a train in Villefranche-de-Conflent bound for Ille, where he retrieved his bicycle from the cargo hold. He pedaled furiously and arrived in Céret a few hours later. As he described in his journal, out of respect for the family, he took a moment to straighten his outfit and put his jacket back on, which he had diligently folded in his side luggage for the duration of the rigorous bike ride. As he stepped into Séverac's home, de Monfreid was greeted by Séverac's parents, and found Violet and Terrus sitting near the bed of the composer. "The poor Déodat is in a coma," wrote de Monfreid. The friends gathered around a table for a somber lunch, but "[A]round 2 o'clock the doctors predict the end," remembered de Monfreid. "Around 2:30, Déodat takes his last breath," surrounded by his grieving friends and family. Manolo later dedicated his sculpture *La Catalane assise* to the composer, whose last words had been, "Music is lovely, I have lived only for her."

Not to be outshined by his fellow artists, especially Picasso, the grand Salvador Dalí, who lived thirty miles away in Cadaqués, Spanish Catalonia, could not resist making a well-publicized appearance of his own in Céret. The proud Catalan native, whose studio overlooked the Mediterranean Sea, had once declared that "The center of the world is this sea and the civilization that was born from it." The event, held on August 28, 1965, had been organized by Dalí himself, his muse Gala, his personal secretary, a few local photographers and journalists who had been warned in advance, and the mayor of Céret, Michel Sageloly. Dalí was dressed in an impressive white suit with gold buttons and plastic shoulder pads, and wore his usual *espadrilles* tied around his ankles. With one of his colorful canes in hand, and his thick dark hair and brilliant mustache glistening, the artist was ready for his close-up.

Dalí and Gala arrived in town in a bright white carriage

pulled by horses, which slowly made its way to the arena as hundreds of spectators piled into the streets, cameras in hand. The Dalian decorations positioned on Place Picasso consisted of a seven-foot skeleton, large butterflies and ladybugs, and an enormous papier-mâché rhinoceros. After an array of speeches by local dignitaries and the obligatory signing of autographs, Dalí walked to the microphone and declared, "My coming to Céret constitutes a historic moment. In the last 10 minutes, I have decided to get married to Gala, a woman I love more than anything in this world, more than gold and money, which is saying a lot!" The celebration was crowned with a sumptuous buffet, and *sardana* dances filled the arena, accompanied by several Cobla orchestras. The mayor addressed his guest of honor, saying, "[I]n this village that has inspired the most important painters of this century, you will find the right place for your resurrection..."

In 1950 a world-class museum was established in order to preserve the extraordinary artistic legacy of Céret. The Museum of Modern Art of Céret, housed in a seventeenth-century convent, which had later served as a prison, is centrally located on the Boulevard Maréchal Joffre near the Grand Café. The museum's founder and first curator, the French painter Pierre Brune, diligently approached artist after artist and convinced them to donate their works of art to the permanent collection. The great masters represented include Picasso, Matisse, Chagall, Manolo, Gris, Herbin, Masson, Soutine, Kisling, Dufy, Marquet, and Dalí. In order to support the museum and add to the success of past introspectives, the Spanish Catalan painter Joan Miró also offered to exhibit his Surrealist paintings in Céret in 1977 and donated two gouaches to the collection. Today, the Catalan village continues to welcome artists from France, Spain, and around the world to experience for themselves the beauty of Céret, even if the decision to visit is based on nothing more than a coin toss.

CHAPTER 5

Music, Monks, and Romanesque Art

*A visit with Catalan painter Étienne Terrus, a close friend of Henri Matisse, in **Elne**, the former Episcopalian capital of French Catalonia—The young Henry de Monfreid (George-Daniel de Monfreid's son and future celebrated writer) and Jean René Gauguin help stage an outdoor play—Front-row seats at the international Pablo Casals music festival in **Prades**—A tour of the Romanesque abbey of Saint Michel de Cuxa—An inspired Raoul Dufy paints his Orchestra series—Long nights of solitary writing for Rudyard Kipling in **Vernet-les-Bains**—George-Daniel de Monfreid's* Le Calvaire *watches over worshippers at Notre-Dame du Paradis.*

Catalan painter Étienne Terrus hosting Henri Matisse and his family in Elne. From left to right: Olga Meerson, Étienne Terrus, Amélie Matisse, Henri Matisse, a friend, and Marguerite Matisse
(From the collection of Odette Traby)

Elne

A 1911 photograph of Étienne Terrus shows the Catalan painter sitting at a large oak table on the terrace of his studio in Elne, in the company of Henri Matisse and his wife, Amélie, their eleven-year-old daughter, Marguerite, and two other painters from Paris. Amélie is sitting next to Terrus, leaning toward him with her hands on his shoulders, a posture that suggests that she feels like Terrus is family. Matisse and Terrus look as though they could be brothers, with their long dark beards, bushy eyebrows, and receding hairlines. Terrus was twelve years older than Matisse. His weathered face and rustic air, his worker's clothes and boots, and his self-sufficient approach to life revealed a true Catalan soul with a deep understanding of the land and its people.

"The Lord of Elne with its cloister in bloom," as his friend the Catalan poet Louis Codet called him, was proud of his roots. The village of Elne sits just over two miles from the Mediterranean Sea, with the Pyrenees Mountains looming in the distance. It is a town with a long and vibrant cultural heritage and a tumultuous history. As the oldest city in French Catalonia and a major stopping point on the road to Spain, Elne has seen its share of battles and takeovers during the last six centuries. Remnants of this past still endure, from the tall medieval ramparts enclosing a portion of the city to the Roman artifacts collected during local excavations. now on display at the Archaeological Museum. But at the heart of Elne is the Romanesque cathedral of St. Eulalie and St. Julie, which was consecrated in 1069. Its beautiful flower-filled cloister, with its short bell tower and elegant arches, was built over the course of two centuries, from the twelfth to the fourteenth, and displays both Roman and Gothic architecture. Today, painters set up their easels overlooking the flower beds while storytellers show young children the shapes of mesmerizing flowers and whimsical animals sculpted into the blue-veined columns of the cloister.

The small village of Elne celebrates its heritage with weekly *sardana* dances in July and August and a popular Romanesque Music Festival each September. The village is surrounded by vineyards, and most of the local residents, grateful for the region's perfect climate, live off the land with rich and abundant market gardens. The year-round market is as colorful and fragrant as the apricot and peach orchards that shade the roads around the village. The narrow streets are lined with stone homes, their shutters closed in the afternoon to keep the harsh sun out or to let their inhabitants better enjoy *la sieste*. These streets are home to art galleries, ironworkers, stone carvers, and glass blowers. The town, nicknamed "La Cité des Arts," continues to inspire creativity, just as it did for Terrus more than a century ago.

Étienne Terrus was born and raised in Elne. Together with his brother, Théophile, he owned vineyards and land, providing him with the security to pursue the unpredictable career of an *artiste-peintre*. Matisse, who befriended Terrus as soon as he arrived in Catalonia in the summer of 1905, was impressed to learn that Terrus, with the support of his parents, had been only seventeen years old when he was accepted at the École Nationale des Beaux-Arts in Paris. Passing the entrance exam was not an easy feat. Matisse failed the test three times and was only finally accepted at the age of twenty-three.

Terrus, however, did not gravitate toward the Parisian lifestyle and never experienced the capital in the way that other artists of his generation did. He rejected many aspects of modern life—reminiscent of Gauguin—and preferred the quiet countryside of Elne. He traveled to Paris half-heartedly each spring starting in 1905 to show his work at the Salon des Indépendants until 1914, when World War I changed everything. Terrus wrote to Matisse in 1912, "The more I travel, the more I realize that only the things you know well can bring you feelings of something new. Traveling is like a cinema to me, where you always leave empty-headed and with a painful back ache." Although he was known to suffer from depression, it's possible that Terrus was simply feeling overwhelmed when he was writing the letter, and longed for the comfort of the familiar rather than the stress of the unknown.

Terrus enjoyed discovering the Catalan countryside. He studied the Mediterranean light with great care, sometimes painting the same subject—like the old chapel of Saint Martin—in the morning and then again in the evening in order to focus on the subtleties of sunbeams and shadows. As one of the first painters in the region to paint *en plein air*, "He possessed early on a musical sense of color and the ability to paint emotions on canvas," according to Jean-Pierre Barou, author of *Matisse ou le miracle de Collioure*. But as a native son of the region, Terrus was not shocked by the bright Mediterranean light the way the newly arrived Fauves painters who came from the dull, gray north were. For this reason, perhaps, Terrus's watercolors were more restrained.

With an easel on his back, Terrus would walk or ride his bike for miles, criss-crossing the region and looking for the perfect spot to set up for the day. He studied the rugged cliffs along the dark blue sea, the tall cypress trees by the roadside, and the local cemeteries. He painted the bay of Collioure, eight miles away from Elne, and finished watercolors in nearby Banyuls while visiting Maillol, whom he had met in the late 1870s. As the sculptor revealed to his biographer Henri Frère, "We were such close friends, we couldn't be without one another." Terrus also painted the abbey of Saint Michel de Cuxa near Prades, where he often stayed at the home of Catalan sculptor Gustave Violet, who kept a room especially for him. As he biked throughout Catalonia visiting his neighbors, Terrus also painted the snowcapped Canigou Mountain from the terrace of George-Daniel de Monfreid's estate. He often took friends—including Matisse—to his small fishing hut on the beach of Racou, near Argelès-sur-Mer, to paint for the day. When his work was exhibited for the first time, at the Société des Beaux Arts in Perpignan in 1882, the press rightfully appointed him "The Landscape Master of Roussillon."

As his reputation grew and local residents started to recognize him as he traveled the region, Terrus, along with Maillol, de Monfreid, Violet, and the painter Louis Bausil, began to organize an exhibit entitled Exposition des Artistes

Roussillonnais, which was the closest thing they had to an official Catalan school. Truth be told, their well-received 1901 exhibit was based on friendship more than on a common art style or movement. They had supported one another throughout their careers in any way they could, whether it was with well-timed encouragement, a bed for the night, or simply a warm meal. Each had his own aspirations, but the men were ultimately bound together by the respect they had for each other and by their passion for Catalonia. As the exhibit returned in 1902 and 1903, there were subtle signs that Terrus would remain a local artist and never become a nationally or internationally recognized name. The press noted that the artist refused to paint large canvases, which made it easier for art dealers to dismiss him. As one critic also warned, Terrus would never gain the recognition he deserved if he continued to isolate himself in Elne. But Terrus never felt comfortable promoting his work in Paris, meaning that his legacy never extended beyond Catalonia.

However, Terrus's ability to live and paint in an authentic way, without concern for proper commercial format, artistic trend, or the next Parisian exhibit, also made him the perfect ally for Matisse, who was struggling in 1905. Terrus was the beacon of Catalan independence that Matisse needed. After the 1905 Salon d'Automne, as the critics viciously attacked Matisse's work, Terrus promptly wrote, "To be bawled out like that, you have to be somebody!" Like a big brother, confident, strong, and without a hint of envy, Terrus believed in Matisse's artistic development.

Whenever Matisse returned to Collioure, the two artists

saw each other almost daily. Terrus introduced Matisse to an old painting technique called *à la colle*, a process that consists of adding glue to water to allow the color to spread more easily on the canvas. Intrigued, Matisse used this technique for his groundbreaking masterpiece *Les aubergines*, which he painted in Collioure in 1911. The friends also traveled together throughout Catalonia. Accompanied by Derain, they visited Girona and Llançà in Spain during their first summer together. During Matisse's longest stay in Collioure, in 1906 through 1907, Terrus boarded a train with Matisse and his wife (who were now in a more secure financial position) to visit the famous health resort in Vernet-les-Bains. They continued on to Prades to admire the Canigou, with its base freshly covered with more than eight feet of snow—so much for the Matisses' attempt to escape the cold.

When Matisse would return to Paris, feeling years younger after a burst of creativity in Catalonia, Terrus was in charge of watching the sculptures in progress stored in his studio and keeping the clay wet. Sharing an update with Matisse, Terrus wrote, "Your heads are not out of the oven yet, the workman needed more coal…and for a few days he had to stop his ovens. You will have them when you return." While Matisse promoted his work in Paris and enjoyed his new worldwide recognition with patrons in Russia, Germany, and the U.S., Terrus would send him small reminders of Catalonia, like a box of nougats from Llançà or a bottle of wine from his friend Bausil's private collection, always showing "a certain sensibility," according to Maillol.

The letters and postcards that Terrus and Matisse exchanged

between 1905 and 1917 show that they discussed personal family concerns as well. When Matisse's daughter, Marguerite, had severe breathing problems that required a second tracheotomy (she had had her first life-threatening operation at the age of six), Matisse shared his fears with Terrus and immediately informed him when she was out of danger. Marguerite had to keep a cannula tube in her throat to help her breathe. She covered it with a black scarf, which can be seen in many of Matisse's paintings of his young daughter. In June 1910, when Marguerite was recuperating, Terrus urgently responded to Matisse, "You could not have made me happier when you told me these two great news: that your crisis of confidence is behind you and that Marguerite's throat is healing. All that there is left to do now is to work unbothered by the opinion of one or the other, always insignificant and fruitless, when we are sure of our honesty, which is the case for you I have no doubt."

When the war erupted in 1914, Terrus was fifty-seven. He retreated to his quiet life in Elne, occasionally interrupted by visits from eager art students who came to his studio to find out the best spots to paint in Catalonia. Maillol wrote that at the end of his life, "[Terrus] couldn't paint anymore, he was trembling. When I saw that he was very sick, I stayed in Elne. I wanted to be with him until the end." On June 22, 1922, Terrus died at the age of sixty-five. The artist's watercolors are his legacy, yet, the compassion, free spiritedness, steadfast support, and loyalty evident in his friendship with Matisse—under the splendor of the Mediterranean light and powerful *tramontana* wind—serve as testimony as well to a life well-lived.

Today, the Étienne Terrus Museum, opened in 1995, is housed near the cathedral. The first floor of the gallery is dedicated to Elne's most famous son and his well-known friends, including Maillol, Maximilien Luce, and de Monfreid, while the top floor promotes a rotating exhibition of contemporary artists who have been inspired by the region. Maillol sculpted a bust of Terrus, which was unveiled on December 10, 1922, and is now displayed on the tree-covered esplanade that circles in front of the imposing cathedral.

Throughout his life, Terrus had had a passion for photography, a relatively new medium developed in the second half of the nineteenth century. He would often take pictures of himself and turn them into postcards to send to his friends. Terrus never painted a self-portrait, but he did build up a valuable collection of photographs taken in his studio, thereby leaving a record of his life and legendary friendships.

Prades

On August 15, 1909, in the village of Prades in the heart of French Catalonia, a three-act play entitled *L'Arlésienne de Daudet* held its opening night. The sculptor and poet Gustave Violet had diligently translated the French play into Catalan for the locals to enjoy, part of his lifelong quest to promote the arts in Catalonia. Terrus had been commissioned to paint the huge theater decor. On several panels of the set, he used the technique of mixing glue into paint that he had recently taught Matisse. When he needed help setting up the stage, he found two unlikely assistants in nearby

Corneilla-de-Conflent—the next generation of Gauguins and de Monfreids. Paul Gauguin's son, Jean René, who worked as a sculptor in Denmark, was visiting George-Daniel de Monfreid and his son Henry. His intention was to stay only for a few days, but the hospitality and the summer activities proved too enticing, and Jean René decided to extend his visit for three months.

Terrus convinced the boys to travel with him to Prades to help set up his theater panels. As de Monfreid noted in his journal, "They make themselves so useful that we stay until 7 p.m. and G. Violet begs me to send them tomorrow morning to help again with setting up the stage display." The unlikely group staged a memorable night for the villagers, who shared an auspicious evening with Paul Gauguin's son and Henry de Monfreid, working hard under the watchful eye of Terrus.

Prades, which has a population of over 5,600, is often represented with the bright pink flowers of the nectarine and peach orchards in full bloom and the snow-covered mountain range stretching up toward a bright blue sky—enough to make even a novice painter want to reach for a brush and palette. The town was built primarily out of the pink marble from the Conflent quarry. This stone forms everything from the sidewalks and decorated front doors to the carved window trims of private homes, some of which are adorned with detailed wrought-iron balconies. The town's stone fountains and old bath houses offer unexpected and colorful details to the attentive passerby. The sun shines all year long in Prades, nourishing the town's vast green pastures, and the weekly farmer's market proudly displays the benefits of the idyllic microclimate. Parishioners congregate every Sunday inside the Church of Saint Peter, which has the largest Baroque altarpiece in France, created by the renowned Catalan sculptor Josep Sunyer. The church was rebuilt in the seventeenth century, and the bell tower is the only remaining piece of the original twelfth-century Romanesque structure.

Violet made his home in Prades, near the Chapel of Saint Martin. He was born into a wealthy family of vineyard owners—so wealthy that the family garage had been built by Gustave Eiffel himself. Much to his family's joy, Violet began his career as a talented architect in Paris, but this was short-lived. Violet soon discovered the arts and traded his career for a life of sculpting, which promptly got him disowned. Violet had an enthusiasm for creating works anonymously, which makes it difficult to accurately survey his accomplishments, but the work that has been authenticated demonstrates his skill not just as a sculptor, but also as a ceramist, a poet, and a playwright. Like Maillol, Violet sculpted large architectural pieces, including the mausoleum in bronze that overlooks the Prades cemetery. His most celebrated piece is the *Monument aux morts de 14-18*, the over twenty-foot tall war memorial combining low-relief sculptures, wrought-iron, and mosaics, which is displayed in front of the Palais des Congrès in Perpignan.

Violet and his friends, known as the "Artistes Roussillonnais," led the art scene in Catalonia and exhibited together on several occasions in Perpignan. Impressed by their individual talent, critics exclaimed, "Hail to Sirs Bausil, Maillol,

Catalan cellist and composer Pau Casals
(Library of Congress)

Monfreid, Terrus and Violet!...They glorified, rightfully, the land that nourishes them." Immortalizing the Catalan worker, the Romanesque churches, the mountains, and the fields of silver-green olive trees, their work served as a testament to the pride and loyalty these artists had for the region.

Although many of today's visitors simply view Prades as a convenient base from which to climb the Canigou Mountain, in 1939 this town was the final destination of a painful exile for the revered Spanish Catalan cellist Pau Casals. By the 1930s Casals had become a celebrity throughout Europe in classical music circles, and was particularly renowned for his recordings of the Bach Cello Suites, the Beethoven Cello Sonatas, and the Dvorak B Minor Cello Concerto, made between 1936 and 1939. When Francisco Franco defeated the Republican government in Spain at the end of the Civil War, the musician was forced to leave his home in El Vendrell and head north to escape the dictatorship.

But why Prades? Casals knew that the villagers spoke Catalan—which Franco forbade in Spain—and, most importantly, that there were many Spanish political refugee camps in the nearby villages of Rivesaltes, Vernet-les-Bains, Argelès-sur-Mer, Le Boulou, and Septfonts. Casals knew that he was not alone in his exile, and he was determined to use his personal resources and prominent name to help those in need. In January and February 1939, more than 500,000 people crossed the border to France, forced to leave their homes and search for a new life, often under dismal circumstances. Casals's lifelong pursuit focused on increasing awareness of the plight of Spanish exiles and the political situation in Spain. He vowed never to return to his homeland while it was still in the hands of a dictator, and never to play the cello in countries that supported the Franco regime.

After a year of renting a house on the Route Nationale 116 at the entrance to Prades, Casals spent the next nine years in the Villa Collette, across from the gardens of City Hall. He practiced the cello every day, composed new pieces, and gave lessons to eager students, some of whom traveled from far away to study under the master. Nostalgic for his home-land, Casals walked past the Canigou every day. In front of the peak, he would pause with his loyal dog, Follett, and give the mountain a wave of his hat.

Music lovers soon spread the news that Pau Casals was now living in the south of France. People wanted to meet the famed musician who, at the tender age of twelve or thirteen, had miraculously found the lost Bach Cello Suites on a dusty shelf in a record store in Barcelona and brought them back to life by playing them in public for the first time twelve years later. In 1947, the violinist Yehudi Menuhin and the pianist Clara Haskil traveled from the United States to visit "Maestro Casals" in the remote village tucked in the Pyrenees. A year later, the violinist Alexander Schneider arrived with a propo-sition that would change Casals's life and the future of Prades forever. He wished to put together a music festival to cele-brate the bicentennial anniversary of Johann Sebastian Bach's death, headed by Casals. However, apart from concerts to raise money for charities that helped refugees in Catalonia, Casals had not played in public since his exile began.

After much negotiation with different groups in both France and the U.S. and intense soul-searching, Casals agreed to lead the festival if it took place in Prades—he wanted to stay close to his companion, who was by then suffering from advanced Parkinson's disease—and if part of the proceeds would benefit a refugee hospital in Perpignan. Casals had already turned down several invitations to play again, including requests to perform at Bach's bicentennial celebrations at the U.S. Library of Congress and in Bach's hometown of Leipzig, Germany. As much an activist for peace and democracy as he was a brilliant musician, Casals was heartbroken that the world was not doing more to fight Franco. Keeping his cello quiet as a form of protest was a small price to pay. It took his friend Schneider to convince Casals to play again and fight *with* his music. As Casals's biographer, Robert Baldock, wrote, "The phenomenon of Casals, after years of silence, playing the full set of Bach Unaccompanied Suites and conducting the Brandenburg Concertos was clearly superb box-office. The problem was that he was doing it in an inaccessible French town no American had heard of."

In the summer of 1950, Prades was transformed. French and American teams had worked hard on organizing the logistics, collecting funds, selecting musicians, and securing a large advance from Columbia Records, which recorded the event. The thirty-five invited musicians arrived, followed by reporters, dignitaries, tourists, and music lovers from around the world. The Grand Hôtel was full, local families opened up their homes, and hotels as far away as Perpignan took in reservations. The surreal setting for such a world-class music festival added to the atmosphere for the musicians, visitors, and local residents alike. On opening night, when Casals finally put his bow to the cello, everyone inside the church of Saint Peter held their breath. The virtuoso did not disappoint the audience. The night was hailed as "the supremely fine music-making of the greatest cellist in the world."

As his celebrity increased and his influence grew, Casals was able to move to a charming home in downtown Prades, a former gardener's cottage on the beautiful grounds of the Chateau Valroc. Casals nicknamed it El Cant dels Ocells ("Song of the Birds"), which is painted over the front door. Unfortunately, the owner of the chateau wasn't always keen on the attention Casals received and often complained about the traffic in the driveway leading to his estate. One day, after finding yet another black limousine blocking his way, the owner had had enough. Someone quickly informed him that Queen Elizabeth of Belgium was visiting Casals, to which the landlord replied with aplomb, "Here *I* am the king!"

Through his music, his work with political refugees, and his travels, Pau Casals fought for peace, for the end of Franco's dictatorship—which he did not live to witness—and for the recognition of the Catalan culture and identity. To widen his circle of influence, however, Casals made an exception to his boycott of Franco-sympathetic countries. He traveled to the United States to play at the inauguration of President Theodore Roosevelt in 1904, and returned to the White House at the invitation of President John F. Kennedy on November 13, 1961. On this second trip, he performed with his close friends Schneider and the Polish-American pianist Mieczyslaw Horszowski, both of whom frequently played with Casals in Prades.

After receiving the U.S. Presidential Medal of Freedom in 1963, Casals accepted the U.N. Peace Medal in 1971 from Secretary-General U Thant who declared, "Don Pablo, you have dedicated your life to truth, to beauty and to peace. As a man and as an artist, you have embodied the ideals this medal symbolizes." Two years later, Casals passed away at the age of ninety-six and was buried in his hometown of El Vendrell in Spanish Catalonia.

The Abbey of Saint Michel de Cuxa

Today the Casals Music Festival continues to draw an international crowd every summer with performances inside the church of Saint Peter and in the exemplary Romanesque abbey of Saint Michel de Cuxa. Consecrated in 974, the abbey is situated less than two miles from Prades. With its tall and elegant crenellated bell tower and its twelfth-century cloister with pink marble column chapters, Saint Michel de Cuxa represents the perfect venue for an evening of music.

The tranquility of the surrounding gardens and vineyards make it easy to forget the church's dark period, which began with the French Revolution. The abbey was attacked and pillaged, and by the late eighteenth century it had been abandoned and sold. Its beautiful cloister was dismantled, and its second bell tower came crashing down after a tragic lightning strike. Over half of the cloister's capitals were taken to New York and were eventually reassembled under the supervision of the Metropolitan Museum of Art. Its Cloisters Museum, dedicated to "the art and architecture of medieval Europe" is located in Fort Tryon Park in northern Manhattan.

During the difficult restoration of Saint Michel de Cuxa, which was spearheaded by Bishop Carsalade du Pont of

Perpignan, several missing architectural pieces, including the arches of the cloister, were found in Prades and Nice and brought back to the abbey. A group of Benedictine monks moved in quietly in 1965. Five monks live there today, humbly offering their homemade jam to the visitors who tour the Romanesque masterpiece. The abbey is now protected under France's Monument Historique designation.

Vernet-les-Bains

Many painters and writers visited Vernet-les-Bains during the nineteenth and early twentieth century. The town was famous for its healing hot springs near the Parc du Casino, which were used in conjunction with its health facility to treat respiratory and severe rheumatic illnesses. In the summer months, the French and Spanish *haute bourgeoisie* filled the grand hotels, and in the winter, the British aristocracy arrived with their Rolls-Royces.

When the painter Raoul Dufy traveled to the south of France for health reasons, his doctor, Pierre Nicolau, invited the artist to stay at his home in Vernet-les-Bains while he received treatments for his debilitating arthritis. The disease, which affected him during the final fifteen years of his life, often forced him to use a cane or, on occasion, a wheelchair. On days when he was unable to get around, Dufy could still set up his easel on the terrace of Dr. Nicolau's home to work on his instantly recognizable effervescent watercolors. In Catalonia, Dufy also enjoyed watching the *sardana* being performed in the town square. The artist diligently recorded

View of Vernet-les-Bains

the details of the dance, first in pencil, and then with paint, sometimes labeling each musical instrument with its Catalan name. He told a friend who had never seen a *sardana*, "You will see . . . it's as beautiful as Bach."

Music helped counterbalance the painter's physical struggles as he tried to live in liminality between pain and creativity. Dufy had developed an early passion for music, listening to Mozart, Chopin, and Beethoven with his classically trained father and siblings. His musicality eventually made its way into his watercolors and oils with his series *Orchestres et quatuors*. Upon seeing Dufy's famous *La console jaune au violon*, one critic wrote that the painting "[e]xecuted in washes of golden ochre... suggests an allegretto by Mozart, whose Rococo spirit, [and] aristocratic and refined temperament, was very much like that of the painter."

Much to his delight, Dufy met Casals at a private concert hosted by Dr. Nicolau in Perpignan. Throughout the evening, Dufy sketched and Casals played his cello. The two artists worked face to face, bringing music and painting together. Dufy was greatly moved by Casals's musical interpretations, which he later interpreted on canvas using vivid colors and a recognizable musical rhythm in every brushstroke. Admiring one of Dufy's paintings, Casals paid him a heartfelt compliment by declaring, "I cannot tell which piece that your orchestra is playing, but I know in which key it is written."

The wealthy British writer Rudyard Kipling and his wife, Caroline, also tested the power of Vernet's waters during a stay in 1910. Fully convinced, they returned in 1911 and 1914. Kipling was enjoying great success after publishing *The Jungle Book* and winning the 1907 Nobel Prize in Literature. Caroline, who suffered from painful rheumatism, spent her days in Vernet taking sulfur baths and drinking sulfur water. As Kipling wrote to his son back in England, the baths were "awful." "I lie on a sort of bed," he described, "where water (hot and smelly) is squirted on me from a sort of garden hose and a man in red and white bathing drawers pounds and pummels and twists and tortures my arms and legs. One feels very slack for an hour afterwards but after that hour one feels very light and comfortable." Some treatments were, it seems, rather painful, including an underwater massage "that makes [Caroline] swear yet makes her better."

In addition to their daily baths, the Kiplings took strolls from their room at the Hôtel du Parc through the town's steep streets lined with hundreds of different types of trees and shrubs. In recognition of this spectacular display in the public garden, le Jardin Nicolau, and the Parc du Casino, and in private gardens—and after a "thorough tree census"—Vernet became the first French town to receive the title of Village Arboretum. For a sweeping view of the village, the Kiplings would climb to the medieval castle and its church Saint Saturnin, a Catalan treasure immortalized by many works of art. The Kiplings also followed the mountain paths on the outskirts of Vernet and walked along the banks of the Cady River, where Rudyard occasionally fished. He was not always successful in this pastime. As he wrote to a friend, "[T]he Cady is full of rude little trout who make faces at me and I don't think I can put up with it much longer." Life in Vernet was simple, centered mostly on "walks and washes." For the Kiplings, their monthlong visits remained "the quietest life under the sun."

Music, Monks, and Romanesque Art

Their fellow visitors included Lord and Lady Roberts of England, who are fondly remembered in Vernet as strong early backers of the town's Anglican Church of St. George, which is now well-attended by the many British residents and summer tourists. There is also the important 1904 *Entente Cordiale* monument, which was built to commemorate the historic agreement between France and England to resolve future colonial and economic tensions through peaceful means. The symbolic monument sculpted by Gustave Violet features two white marble figures, one holding a sword and representing France, the other holding a spear and representing England. Its large pedestal was made of granite "hauled from the bed of the river Saint Vincent [at the Canigou] in carts pulled by oxen." After several unexpected delays, the sculpture was inaugurated in 1920. After being decapitated twice, it stands proudly intact once more, adjacent to the town hall.

The Chapel of Notre Dame du Paradis is a landmark that commands a visit. It is the home of George-Daniel de Monfreid's one and only sculpture, *Le Calvaire,* which stands at an impressive eight feet and seven inches in height and eight feet and eight inches in width. It depicts Christ at the cross with two mourners at his feet, including Magdalen, who was modeled after sketches of his wife, Annette. De Monfreid made his first drawings for *Le Calvaire* in the 1890s, with the young Maillol watching over him.

De Monfreid received much-needed support from Gauguin, who had inspired him to try sculpting. Before

127

giving him technical advice and telling him to "[k]eep the Persians, the Cambodians, and a bit of the Egyptians always in mind," Gauguin shared his excitement in a letter: "I can see that you are in a productive vein; and of sculpture! Admit now, that it's either very amusing and quite easy, or very difficult. Very easy if one thinks only of nature, very difficult if one wishes to express oneself a bit mysteriously—in parables—to search for forms." After receiving a letter from a mutual friend in Paris praising de Monfreid's work, Gaugin shared his excitement with the novice sculptor: "He tells me that...your Calvary is a real revelation—that it is your masterpiece."

The chapel is situated just steps from Vernet's main square, where there are restaurants, a bakery, and a bookstore where visitors can find maps of the local hiking trails. The town makes a perfect base for climbing the Canigou massif and its neighboring peaks, a favorite pastime for Catalonians. A hike made easier with three hundred delicious days of sunshine!

CHAPTER 6

The Catalan Landscape

*Picasso's coming-of-age summer in **Horta de Sant Joan**—Reaching **Gósol** by mule with Picasso and Fernande Olivier—Cubism and the Catalan landscape—Surrealist painter Joan Miró discovers country life in **Mont-roig del Camp**—A visit from Miró's boxing partner, the writer Ernest Hemingway.*

View of Horta de Sant Joan
(©Jean-Pierre Raguenaud)

Horta de Sant Joan

With his long black hair falling over his eyes and his questionable fashion taste, Picasso was like many teenagers and rebelled against the pressures of school and his overbearing father, José Ruiz. Unlike most teenagers, however, Picasso could draw like Da Vinci, and at fifteen he had already won his first honorable mention at the General Fine Arts Exhibition in Madrid for his painting *Ciencia i caridad*. His talent was exceptional, to the point that his father, who was himself an artist and a fine arts teacher at the Llotja School of Arts in Barcelona, handed his brushes over to his son and gave up painting when he realized he could not teach him anything more.

However, Ruiz did expect his son to use his talent and abide by the rules of the Royal Academy in Madrid, where Picasso had registered under the strict supervision of his wealthy uncle, who took care of the boy while his family lived in Barcelona. But Picasso was not a follower. He fought against the restrictive academic teachings, and, as the stress mounted, it was not only his ideas and preferences that came under attack. His body suffered as well, and he contracted scarlet fever. His family decided that he could recuperate in the secluded village of Horta de Sant Joan, where he stayed with the family of his former schoolmate Manuel Pallares.

Picasso had met Pallares two years earlier while studying at the Llotja School before his transfer to Madrid. Pallares was then twenty years old. They often painted together and Pallares soon protected him like an older brother.

Located 101 miles southwest of Barcelona in the province of Tarragona, the quintessential Catalan village of Horta, with fewer than 1,300 inhabitants, had three flour mills and three oil mills, surrounded by rows of olive trees, rye, wheat, almond trees, all enclosed within a protective mountain range. The clean air and healthy lifestyle in Horta helped Picasso grow stronger as the days passed. During his stay at the Pallares family farm, Can Tafetans, he learned the tricks of the agricultural trade with great enthusiasm and quickly adjusted to the demands of living in the country. As a family of peasants, the Pallareses taught Picasso to milk cows, rake manure, light an open fire, and tend to the native white Portenca goats that most families owned. Picasso had always lived in the city and had much to learn about country life.

But before the long list of chores began, Picasso and Pallares celebrated the beginning of summer by taking off to salute the mountain of Santa Barbara, a few miles from the village. They walked past rosemary and thyme bushes, as well as the more exotic lentiscus and rockrose, and arrived at the convent of San Salvador, which stands at the base of the mountain. Picasso made several sketches, which he later adapted in the painting *La processó al convent*. The two friends talked about a longer and more involved camping trip they both wanted to take; the young boys dreamed of going primitive and being free to sketch and paint to their hearts' content.

A few days later, when the preparations for this camping trip had been finalized, Picasso and Pallares ventured deep into the woods. With the help of Pallares's youngest brother and another local boy, they guided a mule loaded with food, easels, canvases, paints, and brushes through the unpredictable mountain terrain. They hiked in the shade of tall Aleppo pine trees until they spotted the perfect shelter under an enormous boulder, their "cave," as they immediately nicknamed it, with a nearby waterfall for their daily scrub. They decided it would be more authentic if they lived in the woods naked, so they stowed away their clothes and turned their attention to painting. After their young guides and the mule turned back for Horta with the promise that they would return periodically to bring food, Picasso and Pallares took their sketchbooks and set off for the picturesque Ports del Maestrat. As they passed a gorge containing a fast-moving river, Picasso, who did not know how to swim, suddenly lost his footing. He tumbled over the rocky terrain, scraping his legs, and headed for the water. Pallares quickly grabbed him by the hand and pulled him to safety. Shaken, Picasso sat on the rocks catching his breath, grateful for his friend's strength and quick reflexes. Many years later, when Pallares made his annual visit to see his now legendary friend, Picasso enjoyed repeating, "I'll never forget how you saved my life."

When they recovered from their fright and resumed their excursion that fateful day in 1898, Picasso began painting the Ports del Maestrat, entitled *Idyll*. His fall had not hindered but rather accentuated the thrill of his boyhood adventure in Horta. His sketches have been saved and are now in the

Picasso Museum in Barcelona, but the canvas never made it out of the woods. It was torn and destroyed by a strong windstorm.

In late August an abrupt change in the weather and persistent rain showers cut short the boys' camping trip, and they returned to the Pallareses' farmhouse near Els Port Mountain. They tended to the olive trees that surrounded the property and assisted in the mill. The manual skills that Picasso acquired and the respect he found for the land, and the peasants who lived off the land, made him declare many times after his visit, "Everything I know I learned in Horta."

After several weeks of work on the farm, Picasso found himself in desperate need of some new clothes. While he lived in such isolation, it took no less than a fourteen-mile "walk"—each way—to the town of Gandesa with Pallares to buy a new pair of corduroy pants. Upon their return, Pallares's mother added to the ensemble when she found two old pieces of brightly colored velvet—one blue and one red—in one of her closets. The boys decided to turn them into vests and proudly wore them around town, much to the dismay of the other villagers.

Amidst creative escapades, farmwork, and some lighthearted moments came an unexpected gruesome encounter during Picasso's stay in Horta, which has left his biographers debating the lasting effects on his psyche and future work. A freak lightning strike had killed a young girl and her mother one night in Horta. To better understand the cause of death, the town's doctor decided to do an autopsy.

He allowed Picasso and Pallares to witness the procedure. Picasso watched in disbelief as the doctor cut the young girl's head from the scalp to the neck. Repulsed, Picasso heaved violently and ran out of the room as fast as he could. One biographer believes the incident explains Picasso's fascination with double heads in later drawings, but another respected biographer dismisses the idea and believes the incident only reflects Picasso's well-known extreme fear of sickness and death. Picasso never discussed the event, only Pallares, but such a brutal scene surely must have seeped into his memory bank and affected the young artist.

As Picasso gained confidence in his artwork and committed himself to a career as a painter, he began to question his signature. He most frequently signed his work with the name Ruiz Picasso, respecting the Spanish tradition of taking both his father's and mother's last names. On many Horta sketches he practiced different possibilities including Picas, Picaz and Picazzo, unsure of how to identify himself. When he finally made his choice, the paternal side of his family was appalled and his father could not forgive him. Later in his career, Picasso revealed that the attraction for him "was the double *s*, which is very rare in Spanish." With his ego and his fame by then firmly in place, he added, "Have you ever noticed that there is a double *s* in Matisse, in Poussin, in Rousseau?"

Still very sensitive to his father's expectations upon his return to Barcelona, the young Picasso brought back an important academic piece from Horta entitled *Aragonese Customs*, which, to his father's delight, won an honorable mention at the General Fine Arts Exhibition in Madrid. Tragically, the large painting disappeared, or, as many experts believe, was simply covered by another large painting done a few years later, at a time when Picasso was unable to buy a fresh canvas.

As biographer John Richardson noted, "Since hardly any of Pablo's Horta work has survived, it is not surprising that this period has been overlooked, despite the artist's insistence on its significance." Indeed, in later interviews both Picasso and Pallares gave memorable details of their camping escapades in Horta. It was Picasso's coming-of-age summer, and he never forgot it. Like any young traveler, Picasso also became proficient in a new language, after speaking and listening to Catalan for eight months. Although Picasso was still feeling pressure from his father and the traditions of the academic world, when he left Horta in February 1899, he was by all accounts a new man and a much more determined and daring artist.

When Picasso returned to Horta de Sant Joan in June 1909, he was once again at a turning point in his life. Picasso, now twenty-nine, was zeroing in on a new art concept. He wanted to clear his head of the noise of the Parisian nightclubs, the endless debates, and the constant distractions. "Our stay in Horta proved to be decisive for Picasso's cubism," wrote Fernande Olivier. After his idyllic stay in 1898, Picasso wanted to bring Fernande, his lover, to Horta to see the village that had become a part of who he was. They settled in the Hostal del Trompet. Soon after, the artist met a young man named Tobies Membranos, the town's baker, who agreed to rent him the second floor of his home to set up a studio. Situated above the medieval arches of the Plaça de Misa, the room looked out onto Carrer de Baix and offered a clear view of the square. Although Picasso had found recognition in Paris and was by then selling his canvases regularly, one of the many appeals of Horta was still the low cost of living. One could rent a house with a view of the mountains for only ten francs a month.

Picasso was thrilled to be back in Horta. As he wrote to Stein, "The countryside is splendid. I love it, and the route leading here is exactly like the Overland Route in the Far West." Unfortunately, Fernande was in great discomfort for much of their stay with a painful kidney infection. Picasso was at a loss. As Fernande put it, "Pablo is no help... When this pain strikes me he becomes pale and that's all—he's as ill as I am." Occasionally bedridden, Fernande distracted herself with American comic strips Gertrude Stein sent to her as well as books, including *The Mystery of Edwin Drood* by Charles Dickens and *Vanity Fair* by William Thackeray.

Picasso preferred to spend most of his time alone in his studio. He began creating some of the most significant paintings in Cubism. As one biographer noted, "Picasso evidently took his inspiration from the landscape in front of him and then manipulated it, playing with the shapes and volumes, so that the resulting picture expresses a thoroughly personal and intimately subjective point of view." Among the many sights he transferred to the canvas was his beloved Santa Barbara Mountain, which he had climbed as a boy with Pallares. The peak is now immortalized in *The Mountain of Santa Barbara*, the dramatic *Head of a Woman on a Background of Mountains*, and *Naked Woman on a Background of Mountains.* The gray reservoir at the edge of town that was used to collect rainwater became *The Reservoir at Horta*, and the simple, square homes of Coll de Sant Miquel appear in *The Factory at Horta* and *Houses on the Hill.* Picasso also finished *Bottle of Anís del Mono*, which features the unmistakable bottle of the popular apéritif.

When he was not painting, Picasso joined in the village's festivities. As Fernande described, "[H]e loved everything that had strong local color or a characteristic odor, which he would inhale ecstatically." He identified with the Catalan culture, which had colored his childhood since the age of eight when the family had moved to Barcelona. In Horta the most colorful festivity is the Feast of St. John, which is celebrated throughout Catalonia. "[T]here were games in every corner of the village and in the main square, too, to the sounds of a drum and a fife," wrote Fernande. "The young country boys and girls danced the *jota*... still great fun as the young people were all fairly drunk." There were also religious processions to the convent of San Salvador at the base of the mountain during which families paraded through town, the children blowing on whistles and the rest of the villagers throwing confetti from their balconies.

Since Picasso's reputation as a painter did not yet extend to the countryside, many people believed he was a photographer, as he walked around Horta with his camera, which used nine-by-twelve glass plates that he stored in wooden cigar boxes. He mainly took pictures of the landscape and the local residents, but he also took photographs of his paintings and diligently sent them to Stein in Paris to keep her involved and interested in collecting more of his pieces. Gertrude and Leo Stein were important financial supporters. Their instincts in avant-garde painting and their insightful contributions as they examined new pieces made them important players. The Steins were more than just collectors; they also became close friends with many of their favorite artists, who counted on their unwavering support to move their art forward.

One afternoon, Picasso took a photograph of a young café owner named Joaquim Antonio Vives, who loved to play the guitar. Picasso later used this image as the inspiration for the painting *The Athlete*. Fernande and Picasso often stopped at the café to play dominoes and chat with the local residents. Picasso would yell, "At your command, Mr. Vives!" They became good friends and sometimes hunted together, bringing back a hare or a partridge. Fernande, dressed in true Parisian elegance, enjoyed the uproar she caused when she sat down at the café. As she wrote to her friend Alice B. Toklas, Stein's partner, "I scandalize the female population with my colourful shawls, particularly the one you gave me." The first time she wore a hat with a small veil attached to it, the villagers thought it was a mosquito net. The fact that Picasso and Fernande had been living together since 1904 but were not married shocked and angered several villagers. One evening, a group of disapproving women stomped toward the inn where they were staying and proceeded to throw stones at their window. They ran away when Picasso emerged on the balcony yelling and waving a pistol in his hand.

Something else kept the young couple up at night. As was the tradition, a watchman, the *sereno*, would walk around the streets of Horta declaring the time and the weather for all to hear. Imagine, as Fernande implored, "a mournful voice waking you up at night:

> *"Praise be to God*
> *The clock has struck ten o'clock*
> *The sky is clear."*

This was repeated every fifteen minutes, the time it took the watchman to circle the whole village.

As the days passed, Fernande and Picasso got to know the villagers, especially the ones who were also staying at the inn. The school principal took meals with them at the long wooden table in the dining room, eating lamb cutlets and mutton soup with saffron. He "infuriates me," wrote Fernande, "because he studied French for a month in Tortosa at the Berlitz school and constantly repeats phrases like: What is on the table? On the table there are some plates and glasses and knives, etc. etc. in his atrocious accent." They also broke bread with the local pharmacist, a young German man who had left his country to escape his military service and "who has never studied pharmacy but apparently performs the functions of a pharmacist miraculously well." Although Fernande struggled with the Catalan language, she found a way to connect, and, much to her surprise, she got along better with the villagers than she did with the people in Paris. She and Picasso often joined the get-togethers that occurred at the café adjacent to the Hostal del Trompet. The café had a player piano, or *pianola*, for entertainment, and the villagers congregated there every Sunday for a night of dancing.

According to Fernande, the chief of police made his men available to them during their stay. She had found the special arrangement quite entertaining. She described in a letter to Alice Toklas, "Can you picture us traveling about the place escorted by five handsome policemen dressed in black,... their uniforms...elegantly brocaded with red, white and yellow insignia?" She told Toklas that one policeman resembled their friend the poet Guillaume Apollinaire. There was also a convict in the town jail who reminded her of the poet Max Jacob, which she found "striking and revolting." The Catalan men in town, Fernande noticed, all wore black or color-dyed handkerchiefs tied around their necks.

Partly because of her lack of fluency in Catalan and partly because she found the women to be "such a bore," Fernande gravitated mostly toward the children of the village for companionship. While Picasso painted in his studio, she spent time with young girls who were fascinated, one can imagine, by her elegant appearance. They would bring her wildflowers and little gifts that brightened her day. She was also attached to a young deaf-mute boy who enjoyed spending time with her. As Fernande wrote, "[M]ost households are blessed with at least one [child] each year."

In early September, Picasso and Fernande said their good-byes to the villagers of Horta and headed to Barcelona, where they began their eighteen-hour train ride back to Paris. According to the descendants of Tobies Membranos, the baker who had rented studio space to the artist, Picasso gave Membranos and his wife a Cubist painting in a gesture of friendship and appreciation for having provided him with such a memorable vantage. His great-grandsons remember Membranos telling them, "The Picasso is hanging on the wall down there in Horta." Unfortunately, this painting has never been found.

Gósol

"Gósol is magical," wrote Fernande when they discovered the remote mountain village in Spanish Catalonia in early June 1906. Gósol, which sits high in the Pyrenees Mountains in Cadí-Moixeró Natural Park at an altitude of close to five thousand feet, had been suggested to Picasso by a friend from Barcelona, the sculptor Enric Casanovas, who occasionally summered there. Picasso's doctor, Jacinto Reventós, also recommended the village on account of its "good air, good water, good milk, and good meat."

The opportunity to leave Paris, where the struggling artist had lived for the past two years, and return to Catalonia had come quite unexpectedly. In early May 1906, the art dealer Ambroise Vollard had dropped by Picasso's studio unannounced, and, in one sweep, offered him two thousand francs for twenty-seven canvases. Vollard had coldly turned down Picasso's work on a previous occasion, but Leo and Gertrude Stein had convinced him to give Picasso's latest work a second

Gósol's inn, now a private residence, where Picasso and
Fernande lived in the summer of 1906

look. For Picasso and his friends living in the crowded and
decrepit Bateau Lavoir complex—complete with bedbugs,
mice, and one communal bathroom—this sudden acknowl-
edgment from the art community was very moving. The poet
Max Jacob fought back tears of gratitude to see his friend's
talent recognized in such a significant way. How reassuring

and exalting it must have felt for Picasso to have Vollard finally take a chance on him.

With this small fortune—a frugal artist could live on a hundred francs a month in 1906—Picasso chose to travel back to Barcelona in style to see his parents and friends, his pride intact. With his revolutionary painting *Les demoiselles d'Avignon* just around the corner, the artist was finally coming into his own and a trip back to Catalonia, back to the source, was critical. As Fernande described in her journal, the twenty-five-year-old Picasso was a different man in Catalonia. "He's more cheerful, not so wild, more sparkling and animated," she wrote, "and he takes a calmer, more balanced view of things... He glows with happiness, so unlike the person he is in Paris, where he seems shy and inhibited." After a few successful days in Barcelona, the couple decided to venture north toward the mountains.

But how does one pass through dangerous mountain terrain to reach what still feels like the end of the earth? Today, the trip requires a train ride from Barcelona to Guardiola de Berga, followed by a thirty-minute drive along a road first built in 1942. The drive, while not especially difficult, does feature some jaw-droppingly steep turns. For Picasso and Fernande, however, the trip demanded sitting for eight long hours on the back of a mule while navigating fifteen miles up a narrow path on the side of the mountain. As golden eagles circled overhead and the sun beat down, Fernande, in a fine Parisian dress and wearing her favorite scent, Eau de Chypre, remained surprisingly flexible during the adventure. As she recalled, "[T]he paths were bordered on one side by walls that scrape your knees and hands, while on the other side the drop is so sheer I had to shut my eyes to prevent vertigo." To make matters worse, as they made their way up the mountain, Fernande suddenly felt her saddle slide backwards, taking her along with it. Her sense of humor intact, she explained, "Luckily I was able to alert the muleteer, who put us all back together—the mule, the saddle, and me."

As they approached the village, which lies tucked into the 41,000 hectares of the Cadí-Moixeró Natural Park, Picasso and Fernande discovered the tall, rugged peaks of the Pedraforca massif, also known by the more descriptive name "Devil's Fork." With its unique double peak, resembling a pitchfork, the mountain looms over the countryside at 8,200 feet. Picasso and Fernande listened as the muleteers recounted stories of witches who head to the top of Pedraforca on the eve of Saint John's Feast and on New Year's Eve for a ritual of dancing and singing, frightening the population below. Picasso, who was uneasy about any superstitious tales, might have preferred to hear stories about hunting and the exceptional wildlife in the area. The region was populated by herds of Pyrenean chamois, wild cats, brown bears, and unpredictable wild horses, which they would encounter up close on their way out of town a few months later to almost catastrophic consequences.

The menacing rock formations around Gósol protrude at odd angles and are quite spectacular. It seems entirely possible that they could come alive at night to keep the witches entertained. Since this region gets more rain than other sections of Catalonia, fresh green shrubs spring with surprising lushness from this rugged gray landscape. This plant growth offers a compelling complement to the rich red Catalan soil and the forested mountains that surround the village in the valley below.

The first mention of Gósol in historical documents dates back to the year 839. The medieval village of Gósol stood on a hill a short distance from what is now the main square. The villagers realized that they needed a flat terrain on which to keep their animals and grow crops, so they eventually relocated a few feet down the valley. It seems the castle already existed by the eleventh century and might have served as a refuge for the Cathars and their supporters. There are several large wall ruins left of the castle, which was once owned by the barons of Pinós during the mid-fourteenth century. Throughout most of the Middle Ages the Pinós family dominated the majority of Alt Berguedá, which is one of three counties that today make up the national park. Adjacent to the castle is the church of Santa Maria, last used in the 1950s. Since that time, the structure has been pillaged, abandoned, and then somewhat restored. Visitors can now enjoy a panoramic view of the impressive mountain ranges surrounding Gósol by climbing a steel staircase to the top of the church tower, where a passionate Catalan flag flaps in the wind.

Most of the men in Gósol in 1906 made their money by smuggling cattle and tobacco (among other, more mysterious, things) across the border to France and Andorra. Consequently, many of them also made great storytellers around the dinner table. Picasso, "like an attentive child," thoroughly enjoyed hearing them recount their adventures. Living in such isolation, the population of close to nine hundred residents survived by growing their own vegetables and by tending to their sheep, goats, cattle, and dependable mules.

Picasso and Fernande welcomed this simple village life. They dropped their luggage in their room on the first floor of the inn Can Tempanada on Plaça Major, the village's main square. The shutters opened onto a balcony, where Picasso set up his easel to paint the row of rose-colored homes across the street, which is known today as Carrer Pintor Picasso. Guests gathered every evening in the rustic dining room on the ground floor of the inn (which was one of the few establishments in the village that had an oven) and sat together at a long wooden table, using local pottery for dishes and water jugs, and eating "cocido," or Spanish stew, with the occasional partridge or hare. Fernande was shocked to find out that the local women did not eat at the table but instead stayed in the kitchen, picking at leftovers. She eventually convinced the owner's wife, Francesca, to come and sit with them. Everyone spoke Catalan, except Fernande, who made do with some well-directed sign language. Today the inn is a private residence with a simple plaque commemorating Picasso's stay.

In his "Carnet Catalan," the sketchbook Picasso carried with him at all times, the artist described himself as "A tenor who reaches a note higher than any in the score." Picasso was in high spirits that summer and was very productive. Although some of his paintings did not survive or were later painted over, we know "El Pau de Gósol," as the artist was now signing his letters, finished at least nineteen paintings during his stay, in addition to many drawings, watercolors, and at least three carvings. He also sketched and wrote throughout the summer, filling two sketchbooks, which are now on display at the Picasso Museum in Barcelona. All the elements conducive to creating something authentic were present in Gósol. Unlike Paris, this village was "untouched by civilization": there were no visitors, no endless debates on art theory, no money worries, and, as Fernande noted, no jealous quarrels between the two lovers. Instead, Picasso was surrounded by the wilderness. He breathed fresh air under the hot Catalan sun and felt grounded and inspired by the countryside. Experiencing a new country or culture can boost an artist's creativity, but a return to one's own roots and cultural values can have the same profound effect. A return to Catalonia gave Picasso the courage to explore the new forms and brushstrokes that would eventually lead to the birth of Cubism.

On Plaça Major, in the center of town, sits a bronze sculpture of a woman carrying two large circular loaves of bread on her head. This work is based on Picasso's *Woman with Loaves,* which he painted in Gósol in 1906 after encountering a stunning peasant girl in the village. The details of her face reveal a new influence on Picasso. During his stay in Gósol, the young artist studied Catalan sculpture, especially the unique piece inside the church of Santa Maria, a twelfth-century statue of the Madonna and Child. The subject is portrayed with simplified features, including wide eyes and penciled-in eyebrows, and Picasso included these details in many of his drawings of Fernande, as well as in his beautiful

Woman with Loaves. Catalan art and, in more general terms, ancient Iberian art influenced his portrait of Gertrude Stein as well. Before his departure for Catalonia, Picasso had painted Stein painstakingly over the course of more than eighty sittings, but he had left the painting unfinished, erasing her face at the last minute. Upon his return, without seeing Stein again, Picasso confidently finished the portrait by painting an Iberian-inspired face, which shocked a few of their friends. Stein immediately accepted it and always insisted, "It is I, and it is the only reproduction of me which is always I, for me."

The primitive setting of Gósol inspired Picasso to try his hand at woodcarving. He requested chisels from his friend Casanovas back in Barcelona, but they never arrived, and Picasso had to make do with his personal knife. It was, however, a very special knife, as he had taken it with him on his first trip to Horta de Sant Joan at the age of sixteen and kept it until his death in 1973. Picasso chose to make his carvings from wood found around Gósol, acknowledging the influence of Gauguin, who had sought out materials that would distance his work from the sophisticated and highly polished European sculptures of bronze and marble. Three of Picasso's sculptures from this period have survived, including the simple *Bois de Gósol*, which is now on display at the Picasso Museum in Barcelona. Picasso also finished a woodcut of Fernande, a work that resembled the well-known pieces that Gauguin had put together for his Tahiti journal *Noa Noa*. Picasso had seen a copy of these travel memoirs through his good friend the Spanish sculptor Paco Durrio, who had introduced him to Gauguin's work as early as 1902.

Picasso had been deeply moved by Gauguin's paintings, woodcuts, and sculptures, particularly the scandalous primitive statue *Oviri*, which he had viewed in Vollard's art gallery. Like Gauguin and many other avant-garde artists, Picasso was drawn to the strength and simplicity of African tribal art. He was fascinated by the many artifacts from the distant cultures of Japan, Egypt, and the South Pacific that he had seen on display at Trocadéro's Ethnography Museum in Paris.

The wilderness of Gósol was the perfect location for the artist to process the works of artists like Gauguin, Matisse, whom he had met at Stein's salon, and "the father of us all," Paul Cézanne. Picasso blended the primal energy of African and Oceanic art with the extreme angles and forms of Iberian sculpture. He added this to his recently acquired Catalan inspiration and found himself on the edge of a new path for modern art. Gauguin had produced his best work in isolation in Tahiti, and relocating to a remote village proved to be similarly fruitful for Picasso. Gósol had unleashed his imagination.

As Picasso created, he also found himself quite content sharing his life with Fernande. He painted her continually that summer. One large nude painting of Fernande, which was purchased by Gertrude Stein upon Picasso's return to Paris, shows the closeness the couple felt at the peak of their seven-year relationship. "[H]er pale terra cotta colored body melts into a haze of pinkish-golden, flesh colored light," described one biographer. This seems to echo Fernande's loving note in her journal. "We have found true happiness here."

Although Fernande was his favorite model during this tender period, Picasso also grew quite fond of the inn's owner, a ninety-year-old former smuggler named Josep Fontdevila. Fontdevila posed for Picasso on numerous occasions and soon became his closest friend. Although he was known for being ill-tempered with most people in the village, he bonded with Picasso and even tried to leave with him when it was time to head back to Paris. Aside from Fontdevila and his well-known temper, most of the villagers, according to Fernande, were quite hospitable and friendly.

When he was not painting, Picasso enjoyed the company of a few men in the village who invited him to go hunting with them and explore the high mountains. On the eve of the Feast of Saint John, the men climbed up the mountains to join the shepherds in building the traditional Catalan bonfire. They roasted goats and shared their "good meat" with the rest of the villagers, who had gathered in the town's square. For dessert the villagers shared the traditional cake Coca de Sant Joan topped with candied fruit and pine nuts, served with Cava wine. The celebrations, which take place in every Catalan village, erupted into singing and dancing and drinking. Picasso sketched as the festivities unfolded, including the important Feast of Santa Margarida, which honors the patron saint of Gósol and is celebrated on July 20. The holiday begins with a solemn procession up the hill to attend mass and ends with dancing and drinking in the square.

Unfortunately, Picasso and Fernande's idyllic summer came to an abrupt end when Fontdevila's granddaughter came down with typhoid. Although reluctant to offend the inn's owner, the artist sheepishly decided to leave. His fear of death and disease, which stayed with him his whole life, stemmed in part from the heartbreaking loss of his seven-year-old sister to diphtheria when he was twelve and from his own scare with scarlet fever at the age of sixteen. When his close friend Manuel Pallares would visit Picasso when they were both in their eighties and nineties, Pallares wasn't allowed to stay in the house because of Picasso's macabre superstitions about aging and death and their possible contamination, even though the two were close in age.

In order to return to Paris, Picasso and Fernande left Gósol and headed north toward Bellver de Cerdaña. The path, known today as the Reaper's Route, is a trail that was used for centuries by smugglers, highwaymen, and the occasional Catalan militia. Picasso struggled to keep his balance on the mule as he carried a small fox terrier Fernande had received as a gift. Suddenly, a pack of wild horses raced in front of the frightened mules. All of the luggage toppled over, and Picasso's canvas tubes, paints and easel, and a small cooking stove they had brought scattered all over the trail.

The heart-pounding accident added to the difficulty of the journey, and both Picasso and Fernande were left shaken and weary. They had left Gósol at five o'clock in the morning and did not reach their destination until six in the evening. They had expected to arrive sooner, but during their lunch stop, Fernande had calmed her nerves with too much white wine. As she recalled, when it was time to go, "my legs wouldn't support me and I had to have an hour's sleep before we were on our way again." When they finally arrived on the French side of the Pyrenees, it was Picasso's turn to feel sick, and they decided to stop for the night. The next day, they traveled to the town of Bourg-Madame to begin their fifteen-hour train ride to Paris.

As his biographer, Norman Mailer, noted, "Picasso will embark on startling new directions soon after his return to Paris." In Gósol, Picasso had replenished his soul and his creativity, and soon the final version of *Les demoiselles d'Avignon* would appear. This painting revolutionized the art world and, for many historians, marked the beginning of Cubism. As his art dealer Kahnweiler poignantly wrote about Picasso's 1906–1907 masterpiece, "I wish I could convey to you the incredible heroism of a man like Picasso, whose spiritual solitude at this time was truly terrifying, for not one of his painter friends had followed him. The picture he had painted seemed to everyone something mad or monstrous. Braque, who had met Picasso through Apollinaire, had declared that it made him feel as if someone were drinking gasoline and spitting fire, and Derain told me that one day Picasso would be found hanging behind his big picture, so desperate did this enterprise appear."

After their memorable stays in Gósol in 1906 and Horta de Sant Joan in 1909, Fernande remained with Picasso through another fateful summer in Catalonia in 1911 while the artist defined Cubism in Céret with Georges Braque. Fernande was by Picasso's side during his most poverty-stricken years, which, interestingly enough, the artist also called his "happiest years." He was not yet pressured to respond to the demands and deadlines that fame inevitably brought. Picasso was still free to explore and define his art on his own terms, guided only by his instincts, his relationships, and his deep connection to the Catalan landscape.

Mont-roig del Camp

"Where I am happiest is in Catalonia, I think the pure Catalan is in Tarragona... All my life has been conceived in Mont-roig, everything I've done in Paris has been conceived in Mont-roig... I don't feel any kinship with the rest of the Spanish people, I feel Catalan."

—JOAN MIRÓ

As a native son, the Surrealist painter and sculptor Joan Miró was fiercely proud of his Catalan identity. Like Picasso, who had moved to Catalonia as a child, Miró periodically needed to reconnect with the land and its people. The artist had a particular affection for the town of Mont-roig del Camp, in the province of Tarragona. In 1911, eighteen-year-old Miró was sent to Mont-roig to recover from a dangerous case of typhoid fever. His parents lived in Barcelona, but they had recently purchased a farmhouse, Mas d'en Ferratge, which stood amidst rows of vineyards and olive groves in the small village. The trip was life-changing. The situation at home had been difficult for Miró. His father did not want his son to become a painter. He had threatened him with two alternatives if he did not give up his foolish reverie: he could either join the church or the army. Instead, Miró had agreed to finish his business studies and was soon pressured into working long hours as an accountant apprentice, leaving little time for painting. Somehow, Miró did manage to convince his father to let him take evening classes at the Llotja School of Fine Arts in Barcelona. But the stress of his schedule, his fragile health, and the constant family tension over his future left him exhausted and severely depressed. To make matters worse, Miró contracted typhoid fever.

Once he was settled in Mont-roig del Camp and found himself free to roam the countryside and capture it on canvas, Miró recovered remarkably quickly. A tenant lived on the property and took care of the farmhouse—a large white house with a tower—with the help of his wife. The farmer's wife soon taught Miró the practical aspects of living away from his parents, such as cooking and making his own bed. He later

Joan Miró
(Carl Van Vechten)

painted her portrait in *The Farmer's Wife* and that of her four-year-old child in *Portrait of a Little Girl*. Miró was quiet and unassuming. Like Maillol, his Catalan contemporary, Miró spent long afternoons sitting in nature, studying "[t]he calligraphy of a tree or a roof, leaf by leaf, twig by twig, blade by blade and tile by tile." He was fascinated by insects like flies and mosquitoes, which often appear in his works. He believed everything in nature, from the tall carob tree to the smallest snail, had the same relevance and should be recognized.

While growing up, Miró did not show an obvious talent for drawing. As his friend Sebastià Gasch once described, "[W]hen he was drawing, he gave the impression of suffering horribly: he used to stick his tongue out like a child struggling to write the first letters of the alphabet." But he was disciplined and hardworking, and he had a teacher at the Galí art school, Francesc d'Assís Galí, who encouraged him to trust his imagination. The artist had a breakthrough when he was taught by Galí to "see" objects using his hands—a process that involved closing his eyes and feeling the object and then drawing it as he perceived it. In 1912, Miró joined classes at the Cercle Artístic de Sant Lluc, which had opened in the famous bar Els Quatre Gats in Barcelona, where Picasso had had his first exhibition in 1900. In class, Miró met a fellow student, the soon-to-be-famous architect Antoni Gaudí, whose vivid imagination would transform Barcelona. At the time, however, Miró bonded with Gaudí over their complete lack of talent in drawing a live model.

Like so many artists, Miró eventually made his way to Paris. He was fortunate to have Picasso, who was fifteen years his elder, take him under his wing. Picasso was helpful to the newcomer in part because Miró was the cousin of his loyal friend and, later, his devoted secretary, Jaume Sabartés. Picasso introduced Miró to his friends and told his art dealers, Paul Rosenberg and Kahnweiler, about Miró's work. Miró looked up to Picasso, as he had experimented with Cubism in his own paintings. The Cubist master acquired two of Miró's paintings and kept them until his death.

In Paris, Miró lived in complete poverty. He later revealed that he used to chew rubber because the exercise of his jaws deceived his hunger pains. According to Miró, he did not need drugs or alcohol because "[h]unger put me in a kind of trance." He confessed that several of his poetic paintings of the mid-1920s were a product of severe hunger-induced hallucinations. But even as he struggled in the early years, Miró took great care of his appearance. He dressed well and stood out from his more bohemian friends. However, he was not arrogant. As he later admitted, "I'm happier going around in a sweatshirt and drinking from a *porro* [wine jug] among the peasants of Mont-roig than sitting among duchesses in Paris in a dinner jacket."

As his career moved forward and Miró found his own form of expression, the artist never lost contact with Mont-roig. Beginning in 1921, he returned to the farmhouse from the summer months through the autumn harvest, looking for strength and a renewal of energy. In Mont-roig, Miró kept a rigorous schedule, dividing his time between painting in his studio, exploring the countryside, and exercising. Although aerobic fitness was not common in those days, Miró could be seen every day on the beach, running, skipping rope, and doing jumping jacks, much to the surprise of the villagers. During the early afternoon hours he practiced "Mediterranean yoga," otherwise known as a nap. Miró also swam in the ocean every night after his work was done.

In Mont-roig, Miró began the intense calligraphy painting *The Farm*, in which he tried to include every piece of the landscape around him, "an inventory of the rural world," as his biographer described. When Miró was ready to sell it at five thousand francs, the American poet Evan Shipmand and the writer Ernest Hemingway both loved the painting and wanted to purchase it. Hemingway recalled, "When I first knew Miró, he had very little money and very little to eat, and he worked all day every day for nine months painting a very large and wonderful picture called *The Farm*." When Miró finished the painting in Paris, he even had a Catalan friend send him grass and herbs from Mont-roig so he could get the details just right. Shipmand and Hemingway threw a dice to decide who could buy the painting, and Hemingway won. Unfortunately, as Hemingway noted, the painting cost "four thousand two hundred and fifty francs more than I had ever paid for a picture." After making a few regular installments, Hemingway could not come up with the money for the last one. Never short of imagination and audacity, Hemingway and some friends went bar to bar begging for money and taking up loans, until he could take the painting home. Hemingway, who at the time worked as a foreign correspondent for the *Toronto Star*, kept the painting until his death, and when his wife, Hadley, passed away in 1979, *The Farm* was donated to the Museum of Modern Art in New York. Miró, who became close friends with Hemingway, remembered the writer as "warm, friendly, and as poor as me ... [To] earn money he worked as a sparring partner for heavyweight boxers ... Sometimes I sparred with Hemingway."

In the 1930s, Hemingway visited Miró in Mont-roig. The white farmhouse with its tower reminded Hemingway of the home he was building in Havana, Cuba. The previous owner of "Mas Miró" had indeed traveled to Cuba, where he made his fortune, and had built the tower upon his return. During Hemingway's visit, the two friends climbed the mountain to the hermitage La Mare de Déu de la Roca and visited the nearby chapel of Sant Ramon and the abbey of Scala Dei. Miró proudly showed Hemingway the Romanesque frescoes and Catalan sculptures that had made their way into his paintings. Miró always enjoyed visiting the nearby village of Siurana, which offered incredible views of the countryside from its perch high on the mountainside.

Miró eventually moved away from his early influences of Fauvism and Cubism to a more poetic style of painting. He embraced the Surrealist movement, founded by the poet André Breton. Breton was a student of psychiatry and had been well educated in the theories of Sigmund Freud and Carl Jung. Miró's *Catalan Landscape (The Hunter)* and the *Tilled Field* exemplified Surrealism's goal of becoming "an artistic response to the power of dreams and the subconscious." Miró insisted that all of the shapes in his paintings were derived from real objects but that they had been interpreted through his subconscious, leaving only, as he described

it, the "underlying magic." In 1925, André Breton bought
The Hunter and called Miró "the most Surrealist of us all."

Just as Picasso had extended a hand to Miró when the artist
was beginning his career, Miró turned his attention in 1927
to the work of a young fellow Catalan painter named Salvador Dalí. Miró introduced Dalí to André Breton and the
group of Surrealists and, soon, hosted dinners in his honor
and invited him to watch boxing matches at the gym. At the
film premiere of *L'age d'or* (The golden age), Dalí's father
took Miró aside and inquired about Miró's opinion on his
son's potential future as a painter. Miró gave a glowing review
of Dalí's work, much to the delight of the young artist. Dalí
had great respect for Miró and his contributions to Surrealism. In 1928, Dalí wrote an article praising Miró in *L'Amiç
de les Arts*, a Catalan magazine based in the coastal village of
Sitges. However, Dalí's political views and his incomprehensible support for Franco during the Spanish Civil War alien-
ated the artist from most of his friends. As one biographer
noted, "Miró made it plain that he detested the human side
of Dalí." Miró had grown up as the Catalan independence
movement was expanding and, as he once declared, "freedom
had meaning for me, and I will defend it at any cost."

After the atrocities of the Spanish Civil War and World
War II, Miró was relieved to finally return to Mont-roig. Now
married and the father of a little girl, Dolores, he was grateful
to return to the peaceful village. Miró, who was by this time
an internationally recognized artist, had begun his famous

series of twenty-three gouaches titled *Constellations*. He finished the last two pieces in Mont-roig, which had been at the source of his inspiration. "During the autumn, on the beach of Mont-roig, where nobody goes," noted Miró, "the human and sheep's footprints look like constellations." As he walked the beach every day, drawing women, birds, and the moon in the sand with a stick—subjects that dominated his paintings until the very end—Miró embodied what he had always hoped to be: the "Universal Catalan."

CHAPTER 7

The Surrealists on the Costa Brava

Salvador Dalí and his wife, Gala, entertain their friends in **Port Lligat** *and sail around* **Cadaqués**—*Gatherings at Catalan painter Ramón Pitxot's house with Pablo Picasso, Fernande Olivier, and André Derain—***Figueres** *and the spectacular Teatre-Museu Gala Salvador Dalí—Watching a bullfight with Picasso, Eva Humbert, and Max Jacob—Exploring Casa-Museu Gala Dali, the medieval castle of* **Púbol***.*

The harbor of Cadaqués
(Jennifer Woodward Maderazo)

Cadaqués

"In spring and fall, the seasons when Cadaqués seemed most attractive, no one could escape the terrifying thought of the tramontana, a harsh, tenacious wind that carries with it the seeds of madness, according to the natives and certain writers who have learned their lesson."

—Gabriel García Márquez, "Tramontana"

"We're going to Cadaqués," Fernande announced in June 1910 to her friend Gertrude Stein. Picasso had decided that "there were too many painters going to Colioure [sic]—Marquet, Manguin, Puy," and had instead accepted an invitation from a Catalan friend, the Modernist painter Ramón Pitxot, to summer on the Costa Brava ("Wild Coast"). "We'll be there until September," confirmed Fernande. "... [W]ith all the Pichot family there will be 18 or 20 of us."

The Pitxot parents owned a large villa near the water's edge on Punt del Sortell, which juts out between the village of Cadaqués and the lighthouse of Cala Nans further to the south. The villa, with its magnificent vistas, was perfectly suited for a festive family reunion. Ramón Pitxot and his five siblings arrived there each summer ready to recharge and catch up with one another. The artistically gifted Pitxot family, in the true spirit of Catalan hospitality, regularly attracted a colony of painters, writers, and musicians in the remote fishing village. To this day, Cadaqués continues to foster a vibrant art scene.

Ramón, the eldest of the Pitxot children, had sealed his reputation as an artist when his work was exhibited at the scandalous Salon d'Automne of 1905 alongside Matisse's and Derain's explosive Collioure paintings at the onset of Fauvism. His sister, María Gay, was a celebrated opera singer who had just finished a whirlwind tour of France; his brothers Lluís and Ricardo were a concert violinist and cellist, respectively. Indeed, the two musicians would one day play with Casals, who became their tutor and friend. Ramón's sister Mercedes married the Catalan playwright Eduardo Marquina, a friend of Picasso's, and his brother Pepíto was the family's photographer and an advocate for the fine arts.

Picasso and Ramón met in the late 1890s when Picasso, nine years younger, began to frequent the Moderniste bar Els Quatre Gats in Barcelona. The two shared common friends in the Catalan Modernisme movement, including Santiago Rusiñol, Ramón Casas, and Miquel Utrillo, who had designed the Pitxot villa in Cadaqués. As Picasso arrived with Fernande, and their dog, Frika, in tow, the summer of 1910 promised joyful evenings around the bonfire and animated conversations about the Parisian art scene.

As had been the case during his previous trips to Horta de Sant Joan and Gósol, Picasso was drawn to the villagers, who provided colorful anecdotes, gave him a sense of place, and inspired his artistry. In Horta and Gósol, the farmers and the smugglers had held his attention. Now it was the fishermen of

Cadaqués who caught his eye. When Picasso was not painting or drawing the colorful boats resting side by side on the beach, he listened to accounts of the local folklore and occasionally joined the Pitxot brothers on a fishing trip. They sailed around the rocks of S'Aranella and Es Currucucu, past the dilapidated fishing shacks of Port Lligat, and put their nets down to catch sea urchins and sardines. Back on the beach, the friends would start the evening's festivities by cutting open the sea urchins and eating this local delicacy with a piece of buttered bread and a glass of bubbly white *cava*.

Picasso rented a studio at 11 Carrer de Poal on the north side of *la rambla*, the main square. Although the house overlooked the sea, Fernande was not impressed. "We are paying a hundred francs a month for a house that has only two beds, two tables, and some chairs," she wrote to Stein, adding, "I find it all pretty awful." Perhaps she preferred the calm mountain air of Horta and Gósol to the fierce *tramontana* wind by the sea. Their maid, who had traveled down with them from Paris, took care of all the cleaning and shopping as best she could without speaking a word of Catalan.

Picasso spent most of his time locked in his studio, "oblivious to everything except the unending task of regenerating cubism." Indoors he painted *Guitariste, Femme à la mandolin,* and *Nature morte avec verre et citron.* He set up his easel outside to paint *Port à Cadaqués* and *Bateau à Cadaqués.* Picasso also worked on an etching entitled *Mademoiselle Léonie sur une chaise longue* to illustrate the book *Saint Matorel,* written by his close friend Max Jacob. According to his biographer, John Richardson, most of Picasso's paintings from Cadaqués are "so difficult to decipher, that even the artist sometimes forgot what a particular image represented." For instance, one painting, still often referred to as *Le rameur* (The rower), actually represents a person sitting at a desk, reading.

On Sunday afternoons, when they could hear music coming through the window, Picasso and Fernande joined the villagers who gathered on *la rambla* to listen to the Cobla orchestra and watch the *sardana*, the riveting dance that had inspired so many artists. Picasso occasionally incorporated Cobla instruments like the *tible* and *tenore*, which are often mistaken for clarinets, into his paintings. "This dance is a communion of souls," the painter once said. "It abolishes all distinction of class. Rich and poor, young and old, dance it together: the postman with the bank manager, and the servants hand-in-hand with their masters."

In August 1910, the painter André Derain and his wife, Alice, joined Picasso, Fernande, and the Pitxot family in Cadaqués. The couple, traveling from Paris, struggled to access the village, as most visitors then did and still do today. Since sea access was oftentimes a more reliable option, the Derains first traveled to Port-Vendres in French Catalonia, hoping to catch a boat to the secluded harbor. Unable to find a ride that particular day, they traveled to Figueres and settled into a horse-drawn carriage, ready for their seven-hour trek. Coming to Cadaqués required "a very steady soul," as Nobel Prize–winning author Gabriel García Márquez noted in his essay "Tramontana." Picasso, who was ever the practical joker, had gone ahead to Figueres to meet his friends and decided to tuck himself discreetly into the carriage, disguised with a black beard. As darkness fell, Alice struck a match to light a cigarette and jumped at the sight of the grinning passenger in front of her.

Derain, who by now had embraced Cubism, settled with his wife on Plaça de les Herbes at the Miramar hotel, which now houses the Perrot-Moore Museum. Side by side, Derain and Picasso painted the boxlike homes of Cadaqués, capturing a Cubist perspective of the low, whitewashed homes with their red-tiled roofs that lay clustered around the dominating church of Santa María. In the evening, Derain, his wife, Picasso, and Fernande came together at one of the restaurants on *la rambla* to toast the day's work and share a few plates of colorful tapas. Fernande wrote, "You would always eat and drink well and plentifully with Derain." The two couples would then climb the steep, uneven cobblestone streets up to Santa María for a clear view of the bay. Picasso told his friends a story he had heard from a villager describing how the fishermen's wives often congregated at the church as they looked out to sea and prayed, waiting for their husbands to come home safely. The church, with its striking octagonal bell tower set on a square base with a single rose window underneath, has since been immortalized by every painter who has ventured to this secluded village.

Later that summer, Picasso welcomed the visit of his friend Frank Burty Haviland, who had been living in nearby Céret in French Catalonia. Together they celebrated the news from Paris that Vollard had decided to stage an exhibit of Picasso's work, showcasing his first decade as an artist and including his work from Cadaqués. Kahnweiler, who was purchasing pieces from Picasso at the time, was less enthusiastic and called his latest works "unfinished." Nevertheless, as Richardson explains, Picasso's "Cadaqués paintings are indeed milestones, in that they constitute the crux of what would eventually become one of the most momentous issues of modernism: figurative versus non-figurative."

Before leaving Cadaqués to return to Paris, Picasso might have caught a glimpse of a young boy running along the beach in his sailor suit. This was Salvador Dalí, then a six-year-old boy, who would become Cadaqués's most famous resident. Dalí's parents owned a summer house surrounded by eucalyptus trees that overlooked the water on Llaner Beach. The young Dalí passed his time collecting stones on the beach with his mother, his three-year-old sister, Ana María, and Lidia Noguer, the owner of the Miramar hotel and a close family friend. He helped his mother in the garden behind the house, collecting melons and plums for lunch, or onions and beets for supper. In the morning he would rest his teddy bear on the windowsill to watch the waves coming in.

Dalí adored "the wonderful little village of Cadaqués, whose every cove and rock I knew by heart, and which embodied for me the most incomparable beauty on earth." But Dalí's peaceful childhood setting hid a terrible pain. Nine months before he was born, his older brother, also named Salvador Dalí, had tragically died before reaching his second birthday. His parents were heartbroken. According to Dalí, his mother's heart-wrenching grief and her anxiety during her pregnancy never left him. His father, a highly regarded notary from Figueres, struggled for many years to let go of his cherished eldest son. Later in life, Dalí wrote with much pain, "All my efforts thereafter were to strain toward winning back my rights to life, first and foremost by attracting the constant attention and interest of those close to me by a kind of perpetual aggressiveness." Having heard about the artist Vincent Van Gogh's similar tragedy with a brother also named Vincent, Dalí proclaimed, "Van Gogh lost his mind because his dead double was present at his side. Not I."

Dalí's passion for painting was fostered by the Pitxot brothers, particularly Ramón and Pepito. Dalí remembered standing in front of Ramón's Impressionist paintings as a nine-year-old boy, gazing "in fascination at the spots of paint, apparently put on without any order, in thick layers, that suddenly shaped up magnificently...Never had I experienced such a sensation of enchantment and magic. That, then, was art!" Soon after, Pepito gave Dalí some paints and a canvas with which to explore his own talent. With his easel set up on the rocky coast, Dalí painted his first oil, *View of Cadaqués with Shadow of Mount Pani*, at age thirteen, followed by *Port of Cadaqués at Night* a year later. "From the moment I awoke, until night fell," recalled Dalí, "I was devoted to comprehending the laws and relationships of light and colors." Dalí was soon ready to commit himself to the profession, confident of his unique genius. The respect and gratitude the young artist felt toward the Pitxot family is evident in his intimate *Portrait of the Cellist Ricardo Pitxot*, which he painted at age sixteen.

By the time he enrolled at the Academy of Fine Arts in

Madrid, where Picasso had studied twenty-five years earlier, Dalí wore his black hair long and was growing sideburns, which earned him the nickname "Señor Patillas." In the summer of 1925, his schoolmate, the Catalan poet Federico García Lorca, traveled back to Cadaqués with Dalí. During this time, Dalí began to grow his now iconic mustache. After playing chess on the beach or reading extracts from Lorca's latest play, *Marina Pineda*, Dalí dragged his friend all the way to Cape Creus, the easternmost point of Catalonia, just north of Cadaqués, where "[e]very rock, every promontory... is in permanent metamorphosis." As you focus your eyes on the rock formations, you can visualize the shape of an eagle, a lion, or a camel, and many of the fishermen have indeed given the scattered rocks such names. Dalí and Lorca walked toward the lighthouse, which had been built in 1853. As they maneuvered as best they could on top of the jagged rocks, they felt, as most visitors do, as though the path was luring them to the end of the world. "This is where my paranoia was born," claimed Dalí, "in this cell of mystery." The two friends surveyed the coastline, observing how relentless and destructive nature had been to the landscape since the insect phylloxera had destroyed rows and rows of vineyards and left the land bare. Dalí would later bring his schoolmate Luis Buñuel to Cape Creus to direct their Surrealist film, *L'age d'or*. The coast was blighted once more in 1956 when an unexpected frost killed thousands of olive trees that had been growing as replacements for the lost vineyards.

After trying his hand at Impressionism, Pointillism, and Cubism, Dalí began to explore the world of Surrealism under the guidance of his early mentor, Miró. Miró was a strong supporter of Dalí and had sent his Parisian art dealer to Figueres to meet the artist and see his work. Around this time, Dalí also discovered Sigmund Freud's *Interpretation of Dreams*, which delves into sexual repression and the subconscious, as well as the writings of Breton and the Surrealist poet Paul Éluard. He poured over the texts of Friedrich Nietzsche and literature from the fields of theology and philosophy. This exploration led to a new direction in his art, his revolutionary "paranoiac-critical method," which he perfected among the tormented rock formations of Cadaqués. "I am a Catalan peasant," explained Dalí, "whose every cell branches on to a parcel of his earth, each spark of spirit to a period in the history of Catalonia, homeland of paranoia." To illustrate this declaration, he liked to describe a bizarre ritual of the fishermen who would hang live lobsters from the angel statues by the altar, only to watch them die during mass and, somehow, feel more passion during the sermon.

Dalí defined his "paranoiac-critical" art as a way to play upon "one's inner contradictions with lucidity by causing others to experience the anxieties and ecstasies of one's life in such a way that it becomes gradually as essential to them as their own." His life formula, as he described, was "to get others to accept as natural the excesses of one's personality and thus to relieve oneself of his own anxieties by creating a sort of collective participation." When you stand in front of a Dalí painting, you are indeed forced to participate. Some viewers find this experience quite uncomfortable.

In the summer of 1929, the poet Éluard accepted an

Salvador Dalí
(Carl Van Vechten)

invitation from Dalí to visit Cadaqués. He arrived with his
Russian wife, Elena Diakonova, nicknamed Gala, their
eleven-year-old daughter Cécile, and a group of friends,
which included the Belgian painter René Magritte and his
wife, Georgette. Dalí was immediately smitten with Gala.
When the group of Surrealists frequented the Miramar hotel,
enjoying cocktails on the terrace, the socially awkward Dalí
would be seized with uncontrollable laughing fits every time
she approached him. One day, while sitting on the beach,
Gala reached for his hand, looked into his eyes, and declared
that she would never leave him. Dalí had found his lifelong
muse. When everyone said good-bye to the Costa Brava, Gala
stayed behind. "Without love, without Gala," the painter
often declared, "I would no longer be Dalí."

Unfortunately, when he announced to his family a year later that he wanted to marry Gala, a divorced Russian woman ten years his elder, his father promptly threw him out of the family home and disowned him. Much like the general public, Dalí's father was shocked by his son's latest hallucinogenic paintings, including the disturbing *Accommodations of Desire* and *The Lugubrious Game*. To break free of his family, Dalí decided to shave his head completely and, before leaving Cadaqués, to bury his hair in the sand with a batch of sea-urchin shells. Unlike Dalí's family, the Surrealists in Paris were mesmerized by the artist's mind and art and urgently invited him to join the movement.

When Dalí and Gala returned to Catalonia after spending a few years in the French capital, they needed a new home. Lidia Noguer took them in and soon proposed to sell the couple two small fishing huts where her two sons kept their fishing gear in Port Lligat. To travel the uneven path to reach the huts on the other side of Cadaqués's cemetery, Dalí and Gala used donkeys to carry their few possessions. They brought gas lamps and heaters, as there was no electricity yet in Port Lligat. Although they were rustic and isolated, the huts suited the young couple. Dalí wrote, "I am inseparable from this sky, this sea, these rocks, linked forever to Port Lligat—which indeed means 'linked port'—where I defined all of my raw truths and my roots." For a while, the only people Dalí and Gala interacted with were Noguer and her two sons, their maid, and the local fishermen. In the evening, when everyone went back to Cadaqués, Dalí and Gala remained alone in Port Lligat.

In his studio overlooking the bay, guarded by the dragon-shaped Sa Farnera isle, Dalí worked long hours, mesmerized by the landscape outside his window. The artist would start working at sunrise to take advantage of the natural light, and then stop for lunch and the mandatory Mediterranean nap, which Dalí called "slumber with a key." He would then return to the studio refreshed and paint until the gas lamp ran out. Gala often spent the evening reading to Dalí while he painted.

Throughout his prolific career, which spanned over sixty-five years and revolutionized the course of modern art, Dalí continued to be inspired by his beloved corner of Catalonia, this "epic spot where the Pyrenees come down into the sea, in a grandiose, geological delirium." Many recurrent symbols and themes in his paintings can be traced back to Cape Creus, Cadaqués, or Port Lligat. As Dalí explained, the idea for the grasshopper motif in his paintings came from his terror of this "diabolical insect" that leapt in front of him, unannounced, every time he leaned on a stone wall to contemplate the view of the harbor.

A more poetic image that made its way into his Surrealist paintings was that of the classical concerts the Pitxot siblings organized out at sea during the summer months. Sitting in their small boat, Lluís and Ricardo played the violin and cello, and Ramón lugged his piano out "on the rocks at Cape Creus so as to establish a dialogue with the waves." Some of Dalí's paintings, including *Partial Hallucinations: Six Apparitions of Lenin on a Piano*, were based on those extraordinary outdoor concerts. The artist continued to reference the piano image in *Skull with Its Lyric Appendage Leaning on a Night Table Which Should Have the Exact Temperature of a Cardinal Bird's Nest* as well as *Atmospheric Skull Sodomizing a Grand Piano*. As Dalí watched his friends playing music out at sea, he became convinced that "Every Catalan is an orchestra conductor who can control and direct the forces of mystery."

The couple eventually bought four more huts, which they renovated over the next forty years. They hired a carpenter and a builder, but Dalí served as his own architect, much to the delight of today's art historians. All the huts were eventually connected, creating a magnificent labyrinth. The huts' roofs were set up as steps leading toward the Mediterranean Sea. According to the instructions, the house was to have no guest rooms. Dalí added a patio and a swimming pool and planted olive and cypress trees around the property. The builder assembled a whitewashed dovecote that Dalí decorated with gigantic forks sticking out on all four sides and large egg sculptures (also recurrent symbols in his work) on top. After years of renovations, Dalí admitted, "None of the palaces of Ludwig II of Bavaria aroused one half the anxiety in his heart that this little shack kindled in ours." When the house was close to completion, Dalí had a long white limestone path leading to their private beach built to run parallel to the sea. Gala planted pomegranate trees, lavender, and rosemary bushes and, her favorite, *semprevives*, or everlasting flowers.

When visitors first walk through the house, past an old wooden boat with a cypress tree growing in the middle of it, they get the sense that Dalí the private man was much less intimidating than the public persona he had created for himself. Although you will never see another home designed and decorated in this manner anywhere in the world, you can also easily imagine Dalí unaffectedly sitting at the long wooden dining room table reading the newspaper or planning his day in the library with Gala and warming up by the fireplace. This was to be his only home, and it provided him with the solitude and peace he needed to create his art.

More than fifty years after they purchased the first huts, Dalí and Gala received an official visit from King Juan Carlos I and Queen Sofía of Spain at Port Lligat in 1981. Loyal to his native land until the end, Dalí would eventually leave his paintings and his entire fortune to the Spanish state. After some litigation, Cécile Éluard, Gala's daughter, who had been practically abandoned by her mother and stepfather, was also awarded a sizable inheritance.

Figueres

Surrounded by vineyards, sought-after cork oaks, and elegant cypress trees, Dalí's hometown of Figueres emerges from the plain of Ampurdan as the agricultural center of Spanish Catalonia. Nineteen miles inland from the rugged seascape of Cadaqués, Figueres is the capital of Alt Empordá County, in the province of Gerona, and is home to nearly 20,000 residents. At 6 Carrer Monturiol, a street named after the inventor of the first combustion-powered submarine, Salvador Dalí was born on May 11, 1904. His father, a respected notary, hoped his son would follow in his footsteps, but the young

Dalí was soon playing with watercolors. "[F]rom the balcony of my father's house looking down on all Figueres," Dalí recalled, "I could see the plain of Ampurdan and the Gulf of Rosas, from which the calls to my vocation came to me and allowed me to escape from the bourgeois notarial universe." While in school, Dalí finished one of his earliest watercolors. The painting represented the beautiful Romanesque church of Santa María de Vilabertrán, which was visible from the window of his classroom. Impressed by his son's sophisticated draftsmanship, Dalí's father occasionally sent the boy to the Pitxot estate, El Molí de la Torre ("The Tower Mill"), on the outskirts of Figueres, to spend time with Ramón Pitxot.

The heart of Figueres, as in all Catalan towns, is *la rambla*. Lined with plane trees, the central promenade is alive with cafés and bistros. The square brings villagers together on market day and attracts thousands of visitors with a popular antique market each month on Plaça del Gra. Nearby stands a Noucentista memorial by Picasso's friend, Enric Casanovas, which honors Monturiol. The local café life, where people catch up, eat and drink together, and watch the world go by, was important to Dalí, who favored what he called "ultralocalism." As he explained, "In Figueres there is a small café that fancies itself headquarters for the sporting crowd, known as Sport Figuerense. A good share of my doings are aimed solely at that spot: I act in terms of what people there will say about me. International opinion means less to me than their reactions!" Sitting with friends at the Café Royal—today the Hotel Café Paris—Dalí and his schoolmate Luis Buñuel wrote the screenplay for their first Surrealist film, *Un Chien*

Andalou (An Andalusian dog). Dalí also dined regularly at the Hotel-Restaurant Duran, which has been open since 1855. In time, he was given his own private room in the back. As the owner, Lluís Duran, recalled, eccentricity was always part of his visits. Dalí once ordered a bowl of soup and threw it in the air, just to catch the attention of his fellow diners. On one occasion, he arrived on a hot summer day wearing the Catalan *barretina* on his head, his regular black canvas espadrilles tied around his ankles and an incongruous long mink fur coat. Keeping his sense of humor intact, Duran became friends with the artist. Dalí often came around the restaurant after a trip abroad, nostalgic for his traditional Catalan cuisine.

As Dalí dined at Duran's one evening in 1961, the mayor of Figueres approached the artist with the idea of building a museum in Dalí's honor. Together they discussed the possibility of renovating the old theater, which had been severely damaged during the Civil War of 1936–1939. The place held special meaning for Dalí, since he had participated in his first exhibition there in 1918, alongside thirty other artists from Gerona and Barcelona. He was only fifteen years old at the time, but, as he sold his first Impressionist paintings, two critics declared in the press that Dalí was "one of those artists who will cause a great sensation...one of those who will produce great pictures...We welcome this new artist and express our belief that at some point in the future our humble words will prove to be prophetic."

When the plans for the Teatre-Museu Salvador Dalí were finalized, the artist realized that "Nothing could suit me

The Gala-Salvador Dalí Theater-Museum
(Erin Silversmith)

better than a theater as setting for the facets of my caprices. This was to be no ordinary museum!" Promising to create a place "in a state of permanent unveiling," Dalí worked tirelessly on his creation until the grand opening in 1974. It is exciting to imagine Dalí walking around with his cape and cane during the renovations. He must have explained to his entourage how to set up Al Capone's Cadillac in the circular courtyard and pointed out the spot where visitors would be able to drop coins in a box to make it "rain," soaking the ceramic snails inside. His workers would have frantically nodded in agreement, taking notes and trying desperately to keep up with the witty and brilliant Maestro. It must have been surreal indeed for everyone involved. Each creation inside the museum (and there are many spectacular ones) can be interpreted in different ways. One historian believes the decorations on the striking dark red walls of the theater represent "turds" while another historian describes them as "Catalonian weaved round breads." According to Dalí's instructions, they are indeed loaves, but the artist would surely have reveled in the confusion.

Dalí spent the last five years of his life in seclusion inside the Galatea Tower, adjacent to the theater. The tower is topped with large egg sculptures, which are visible from far away. Standing proudly on Plaça Gala-Salvador Dalí, at the entrance of the now most-visited museum in Spanish Catalonia, a statue rises and declares, "The Catalan spirit rejects and outlives its gravediggers."

Púbol

When "Avida Dollars"—an anagram nickname Breton created to mock Dalí's greed and newfound success in the United States—promised to buy his beloved Gala her own castle, he pulled out all the stops in looking for the best possible property, even recruiting an airplane and a photographer for this important mission. Gala eventually chose the medieval castle of Púbol, located twenty miles south of Figueres. The castle, which had been built in the fourteenth century along with the adjacent church of Saint Peter, had been neglected and needed significant renovations. The property was spotted with fig and cypress trees, as well as ivy, jasmine, and blackberry bushes. Gala was drawn to the castle's air of mystery. She admired the century-old plane trees that guarded the entrance and the colorful rose bushes that grew on the side of the wall and which reminded her "of a garden in Crimea where she used to spend her summer holidays as a child." Dalí and Gala had an affinity for the village of Púbol, as it was near the Sanctuary of Els Angels, where the couple had married in a Catholic ceremony on August 8, 1958.

Gala wanted the castle, with its romantic interior courtyard, to be "monkish." "I like solitude and simplicity," Gala said. "In Dalí's house everything is overblown." After being surrounded by Dalí's eclectic furnishings for the past forty years, Gala decorated the private rooms of her castle sparsely, adding select souvenirs from Russia, such as her books and photographs. She did, however, make impressive lists of requests for Dalí. She wanted the ceiling of the vestibule to be painted and required "a 15-metre panel representing in the Mediterranean sky a nocturnal hole out of which fall the Surrealist treasures." Gala shopped for antiques throughout Catalonia and, as a final touch, made sure that every room, including her blue bedroom and the crimson guest room, had a large yellow bouquet of dried everlasting flowers.

During the renovations, which ended in the summer of 1970, Dalí found ways to add his personal touch to the property. In the garden, among the fig and cypress trees, he installed four eccentric cement sculptures of elephants with skinny storks legs. Inside the castle, Dalí drew many sketches with the builder, and eventually "[t]he piano-fountain, the sofa lips, the elephant with obelisk, the anthropomorphic sofa, the designs for table lamps and so on were integrated, at least partially, into the world of Púbol." Still, Dalí insisted that everyone know and acknowledge that this was Gala's castle. She thanked him for his gift and declared, "I will accept the Castle of Púbol, but only on one condition, that you will not come to visit me at the castle unless it is with a written invitation."

From 1970 to 1981, Gala stayed at the castle primarily in the summer, and never for longer than three weeks at a time. Over the years she acquired a reputation for hosting numerous parties and lovers in Púbol, including her ex-husband, Éluard, and lavishing her company with expensive gifts. A few weeks before her death in 1982, as Dalí faced the prospect of losing her, the artist had a crypt installed. His wife was buried there on June 11. Dalí did not attend the ceremony, but was seen by a maid weeping at her tomb hours later, when the guests had left. Soon after, the king of Spain bestowed upon him the title of Marquis de Púbol, which is engraved on his tombstone in Figueres. Dalí had been elevated to the status of nobility, which seemed appropriate since, during the renovations of the castle, he had been designing a baroque-style throne from which to better receive the press.

Dalí stayed in Púbol until August 31, 1984, when a fire broke out in his bedroom and injured him severely, both mentally and physically. Dalí had clicked one too many times on the servant's bell. The mechanism caused a short circuit that caught Dalí's silk sheets on fire and engulfed the room in flames. Dalí was brought to a hospital in Barcelona where he endured painful skin grafts on his leg. He abandoned Púbol with a heavy heart and settled in the Galatea Tower in Figueres, eventually disappearing from public life.

When the artist passed away on January 23, 1989, a grand funeral took place at the Gothic church of Saint Peter across the street from the Theater-Museum in Figueres. Following the ceremony, Dalí was buried in an underground crypt inside the museum. A few days after her brother's death, Ana María invited the villagers of Cadaqués to a special mass at the church of Santa María to remember the great Salvador Dalí and his "delirium battered on the dreamlike anguishes and mysteries created by the interplay of winds, rocks, and sea."

CHAPTER 8

Sun, Sky, and Sand

*Spanish Catalan painters Santiago Rusiñol, Ramon Casas, and Miquel Utrillo in **Sitges** and the Catalan Modernisme movement—Picasso and his friend Carles Casagemas's last visit with family before tragedy strikes—Hiking along the crenellated towers and ramparts of **Tossa de Mar** in the footsteps of Marc Chagall and his "blue paradise."*

Marc Chagall

Tossa de Mar

Twenty miles south of Girona in Spanish Catalonia, Tossa de Mar emerges at the end of a long, winding road, rewarding visitors with exceptional views of the sapphire blue sea and the rugged cliffs of the Costa Brava. In 1934, the year their daughter Ida married, the painter Marc Chagall and his wife, Bella, decided to escape the prewar tensions in Paris by spending their summer in the quiet fishing village of Tossa, which lies halfway between Barcelona and the border of French Catalonia.

The couple met in 1909 in their hometown of Vitebsk, Belarus—at the time still part of Tsarist Russia—and were soon engaged. Chagall was already enrolled in art classes, but pursuing his desire to become an artist had not been easy. "[A] word as fantastic, as literary, as otherworldly as the word 'artist,'" wrote Chagall, "well...it had never been uttered by anyone in our town." One afternoon, a schoolmate had walked into his room and admired his drawings hanging on the wall, calling Chagall "a real artist." The young Chagall was speechless. He dreamed of taking local art classes and one day, as his mother baked in the kitchen, he summed up all his courage and cried out, "I wish to be a painter. Save me, Mamma. Come with me... there's a place in town; if I'm admitted, and I finish the course, I'll be a complete artist by the time I leave. I should be so happy!" His mother frowned. "What? A painter? You're mad!"

After some persuasion, Chagall joined Vitebsk's School of Painting and Design. "I was the only one to paint in violet," Chagall remembered. "Where does that idea come from?" he wondered. He soon mesmerized the art world in Paris with his unique style of painting, described as "supernatural" by his friend and French poet Guillaume Apollinaire.

During the summer of 1934, in Tossa, Chagall was inspired by the Mediterranean Sea and the region's vibrant light. He named the village his "blue paradise." The artist was a master of color and often returned to familiar themes in his paintings, like bouquets of flowers and whimsical animals such as cows, cheerful donkeys, and roosters. These elements were interspersed with souvenirs of Russia's countryside and a touch of "Eastern European Jewish folk culture." Picasso declared in the 1950s, "There's never been anybody since [Pierre-Auguste] Renoir who has the feeling for light that Chagall has," adding, "[W]hen Matisse dies, Chagall will be the only painter left who understands what color really is."

In the evenings, Chagall and Bella walked through the old district, Vila Vella, which is situated on a long stretch of rugged cliffs along the Mediterranean Sea. The labyrinth of narrow cobblestone streets is completely enclosed by twelfth- and fourteenth-century city walls. This archaeological preservation makes the medieval town the pride of local residents, as it is unique on the Spanish Catalan coast. The ramparts are linked by watchtowers, high on the promontory, with views of Tossa's largest beach Platja Gran and the new district called Vila Nova, where most of today's 4,000 residents live.

It's easy to imagine the master of fantasy and his loving wife carrying a dinner picnic up to the old lighthouse, built in 1917, to enjoy a magical sunset amid the forest of pine trees. They might have reminisced about the many travels they had enjoyed together through Russia, Italy, Paris, and Spain. The 1920s had been good to them. Chagall's paintings had been selling well, thanks to a fruitful contract with Kahnweiler. Chagall's days of buying a mere piece of cucumber at the market, as he recalled in his memoirs, were firmly behind him.

As Chagall's talent became internationally recognized, the artist was reluctant to admit that he had put aside painting completely for a time. While on a return visit to his hometown in the early 1920s, the artist had accepted the post of Minister of Arts of Vitebsk. His wife had urged him not to neglect his painting and did not believe the position would make him happy. As it turned out, she was right. Chagall later wrote, "She warned me that it would all end in insults, in snubs. It was so." He added lightheartedly, "[U]nfortunately, she is always right. When will I learn to take her advice?"

Bella and Marc Chagall had a very loving and supportive relationship, and Chagall suffered greatly when he lost his soul mate unexpectedly in 1944. Chagall often painted the couple floating on the canvas, holding hands or kissing, such as in *La promenade, Au-dessus de la ville, L'anniversaire,* and the whimsical *Double portrait avec un verre de vin,* which shows the two lovers "intoxicated with happiness."

Although the mood of the country had changed by the

1930s, with Hitler's rise to power in Germany and anti-Semitism spreading across Europe, Chagall still found some joy in Tossa. As he wrote to Kahnweiler, "I'm happy to write to you that Tossa is paying off in my work. The countryside that surrounds it is beautiful." A couple of months later, he confessed, "I love this homeland, I wish to stay in Tossa for as long as possible."

To savor the town's atmosphere after a day's work inside the studio, where Bella occasionally posed for her husband, the couple walked the length of the beach, past the colorful boats pulled up to shore and up to the fishermen's quarter known as Sa Roqueta. Although he was a discreet man, Chagall enjoyed getting to know the local residents. He acknowledged years later that "It's nice to know that I have friends in the country of Cervantes and Goya." The neighborhood Sa Roqueta had been built in the sixteenth century, when Tossa began to expand outside the medieval ramparts of Vila Vella. Today, the streets come to life on June 5 for Fishermen's Day, when the villagers celebrate their maritime heritage by eating salty sardines for breakfast on the beach and drinking *cremat*, a coffee spiked with rum. The fishermen then belt out traditional sea chants called *havaneres* until the whole village is singing along.

One day during Chagall's visit to Tossa de Mar, the mayor approached the artist to discuss a plan to build a Municipal Museum to celebrate the works of nineteenth- and twentieth-century painters who had made their home on the coast and to house the archaeological treasures found during the expansion of the village. Chagall supported the idea and donated one of his paintings, *The Celestial Violinist.* The piece now hangs radiantly in the former governor's house on Plaça del Pintor Roig y Soler in Vila Vella. In September 1935, the villagers celebrated the opening of the first contemporary art museum in Spain and paid homage to Marc Chagall's luminous stay in Tossa de Mar.

Sitges

Sitges, with its enchanting sun-drenched coast, is situated on the southern Costa Dorada, twenty-five miles south of Barcelona. Protected by the Garraf Mountains, the village showcases a stunning seventeen beaches. At the heart of Sitges is the seventeenth-century church of Sant Bartomeu i Santa Tecla, which stands defiantly on the rocky promontory La Punta, overlooking the Mediterranean Sea. Its octagonal bell tower, photographed by all who visit, is crowned by a large sculpture of the Virgin Mary. Inside, visitors are drawn to the elaborate central altarpiece, which features the two patron saints for whom the church is named. As in many churches in small towns throughout Catalonia, the baroque altars were built to such high standards that most have survived beautifully through wars and conflicts.

Behind the church of Sant Baromeu i Santa Tecla is a wondrous maze of narrow pedestrian streets running through the Old Quarter. The whitewashed homes, including nearly eighty breathtaking Modernista villas, bring out a nineteenth-century feel with their elegant arches, entranceways detailed with relief work, Art Nouveau stencils on the walls, and wrought-iron balconies covered with fresh flowers taking in the light. Many of these homes on Carrer de l'Illa de Cuba, Sant Gaudenci, Sant Isidre, and Francesc Gumá were built by wealthy Barcelonians who escaped to the coast for their holidays.

In the eighteenth century, ambitious Catalans immigrated to Cuba and Puerto Rico when the trade restrictions between Spain and the American colonies were lifted, allowing for the export of wines and other commodities. When *los Americanos* returned to Catalonia with full coffers, they were eager to embellish their villas with the latest textiles, arts and crafts, and lavish woodworks inspired by the current Modernisme movement. The movement began in the late 1880s and was described as "Catalan art nouveau with overtones of symbolism." The decorative style incorporated the elegant lines found in Japanese art into furniture design, moldings, fireplaces, and terraces. Artisans were inspired by nature and turned to the use of raw materials like wrought iron, steel, glass, and precious metals. They created colorful glass mosaics and painted tiles, which were very popular for both exteriors and interiors.

The movement soon became a beacon of Catalan pride. It embodied the region's progressive attitudes toward art and architecture, which were more on par with those of European cultures than with that of the rest of Spain. The Modernista painters in particular shared a desire to break free from traditional painting and broaden "their range of subjects to include prostitutes, beggars and the peasants—and not just the upper classes or religious allegories" that had been so prevalent in academic circles.

One of the premier Modernista painters and the heir to a successful textile factory, Santiago Rusiñol, is remembered in Catalonia as "a public-spirited impresario." While the newly sought-after Modernista architects Antoni Gaudí, Josep Puig i Cadafalch, and Lluis Domènech i Montaner were revolutionizing the landscape of nearby Barcelona, Rusiñol was laying out the groundwork in Sitges. In 1891, the artist purchased two fishing cottages and transformed them into a new home and studio for himself "using the remains of Sitges' medieval castle." He called it Cau Ferrat, and it soon became a bustling meeting place and cultural center for young artists throughout Catalonia. During evening gatherings, Rusiñol entertained guests at his grand piano as they admired his vast collection of paintings, ceramics, woodcarvings, stained glass, and forged ironwork, for which the home was named.

Rusiñol joined forces with the Luminist School, a group of Catalan landscape artists already established in Sitges. With this group, which included Arcadi Mas i Fontdevila, Joaquim de Miró, and Joan Roig i Soler, Rusiñol began to organize the first Modernisme Festival. Writers, sculptors, painters, art critics, and musicians all converged on the small coastal town to attend exhibits, critique one another's work, and join in the conversation on what Modernisme could mean for Catalonia. Rusiñol declared to the crowd of supporters, "We prefer to be symbolists and unstable, and even crazy and decadent, rather than fallen and meek...Common sense oppresses us; there is too much cautiousness in our land."

The hugely successful Modernisme Festival returned in 1893 and 1894 and propelled Sitges to the forefront of the

Statue of Santiago Rusiñol
(©Jean-Pierre Raguenaud)

movement. Rusiñol was joined by his friends and fellow Catalan artists Ramon Casas and Miquel Utrillo, who were both leaders of the new aesthetic movement. As the artists gathered on the blue terrace of Cau Ferrat, Utrillo took the time to share intriguing personal news with his friends in between intellectual conversations on how to rejuvenate Catalan art and culture. The artist had recently acknowledged paternity of a young boy named Maurice. His mother, the famous young Parisian model and artist Suzanne Valadon, had posed for Puvis de Chavannes, Pierre-Auguste Renoir, Edgar Degas, and Henri de Toulouse Lautrec, and could not be certain of the identity of the boy's true biological father. Utrillo had settled the paternity issue by telling Valadon, "I would be glad to put my name to the work of either Renoir or Degas!"

Utrillo left a remarkable legacy in Catalonia as an architect and interior designer of the Modernisme movement. In particular, Utrillo contributed to the charm of Sitges when a wealthy American art collector, Charles Deering, hired him to take charge of the renovations of a building that he had purchased near Cau Ferrat. Named Palau Mar-i-cel ("Palace of Sea and Sky") by Utrillo, the three-story building was a former hospital that had been built in the fourteenth century. The exterior was whitewashed and adorned with carved relief artwork around the windows and doors. The stunning cloister terrace, which overlooked the sea and opened to the sky, was transformed with magnificent tiles depicting the Catalan countryside. The Palau Mar-i-cel is now open to visitors only in the summer and is used for cultural events and receptions during the rest of the year.

Once his personal art collection was put on display, Deering then realized his living quarters had to be expanded. He purchased the building next door, and Utrillo built a beautiful covered walkway above street level in between the two buildings. A large portrait of Deering, painted by Casas, welcomes visitors into the vestibule. The former family home now houses the art museum Maricel de Mar, which features a collection of paintings from artists connected with Sitges. The details in the design of each room make the house itself a work of art. Leaning against the town's high seawall, the home includes a large bright gallery with floor-to-ceiling windows that open up on the clear Mediterranean Sea—a perfect backdrop for the stunning nineteenth-century sculptures it contains.

Together with Utrillo and Rusiñol, the painter Casas is recognized as an illustrious figure of "Catalan Modernisme." Casas first worked as a writer and illustrator for the Catalan magazine *L'Avenç*, where the term Modernisme first appeared in 1884. An excellent draftsman, Casas built a reputation as one of the best and most sought-after portraitists in Catalonia. Born to a wealthy family and one of the first people to own a car in Barcelona, Casas opened the legendary Els Quatre Gats tavern with Rusiñol, Utrillo, and their friend Pere Romeu, who served as host. With a large self-portrait of Casas smoking a pipe and Romeu pedaling a tandem bicycle hanging over the bar, the friends welcomed young painters, playwrights, and musicians and organized regular art exhibitions to showcase the latest trends.

When the Modernisme Festival returned to Sitges in 1897 and, for a final time, in 1899, the young Picasso kept abreast of the developments in the magazine *L'Avenç*. Much of Picasso's early work, from 1897 to his Blue Period in the early 1900s, stemmed from Catalan Modernisme. Picasso frequented Els Quatre Gats and occasionally designed restaurant menus, posters, and illustrations for the local exhibits. He became close friends with regulars at the tavern, including the sculptor Manolo Hugué and the painters Joaquim Sunyer and Carles Casagemas. Recognizing Picasso's early talent, Rusiñol, Casas, and Utrillo hosted his first solo exhibit at the tavern in February 1900.

As Picasso and Casagemas planned their first visit to Paris in the fall of 1900, the two friends decided to travel first to Sitges to visit with Casagemas's family. His father, the American Consul General of Barcelona, owned a villa on the water's edge, where Casagemas had spent many summers as a child. His friend Hugué remembered Casagemas as a generous man who always dressed elegantly. When Hugué voiced his desire to move to Paris, "the undisputed center of international art," Casagemas had immediately promised him financial support. But it was not to be.

While in Sitges, Picasso and Casagemas visited Rusiñol, who gave them a tour of Cau Ferrat. Rusiñol pointed out his large collection of tiles, some dating from the fifteenth century, which ornamented the home's stairs, columns, and deep blue walls, as well as its large terrace overlooking the bay. Picasso sat down with Rusiñol in the studio on the ground floor to do a charcoal portrait of him, which is now on display in Sitges along with three other drawings and one early painting entitled *La course de taureaux*. One evening at a tavern, Picasso and Casagemas ordered drinks to celebrate their upcoming trip to Paris. Picasso, who was not quite twenty years old at the time, had been chosen to have one of his paintings, entitled *Les derniers moments,* put on display in the Spanish Pavilion at the World's Fair. (The work has recently been found under his 1903 painting *La vie* with the use of X-rays.)

Casagemas, on the other hand, did not seem well in Sitges. As Picasso later told his biographer Richardson, when they headed out one night, "Casagemas insisted on going to the cemetery to paint, but none of the vistas suited him. They ended up in the family villa, where Casagemas persuaded Picasso to sit for his portrait. After some time, Picasso got up to see the result: Casagemas had done absolutely nothing." Picasso was unsettled, but he could not have foreseen that six months later Casagemas would be dead from a self-inflicted gunshot wound. The tragedy, which became legendary in artistic circles, unfolded after a brief romance in Paris with a woman named Germaine (who would later marry Ramón Pitxot). When she refused to pursue a relationship with him, Casagemas attempted to kill her as they dined with friends then turned the gun on himself. Picasso was devastated. He had considered Casagemas his closest friend and was suddenly forced to face the difficult subjects of mortality and human suffering on a very personal level. Picasso entered what is now recognized as his Blue Period with a portrait of Casagemas called *Évocation ou l'enterrement de Casagemas.* As one historian observed, as a consequence of Casagemas's suicide, "Picasso sought redemption... by creating a vast world of sexuality, strength, and virility. The specter of death, and his need for redemption and survival, haunted Picasso into his 90s."

*　　*　　*

Sitges was also the home of Picasso's friend the Catalan painter Joaquim Sunyer, whose uncle, Joaquim Miró, had been a member of the local Luminist school. Like many dedicated artists, Sunyer had moved to Paris to study the great masters at the Louvre. He took art classes at a reputable academic studio and, at night, shared a *pastis* with fellow Catalan artists, hungry for intellectual stimulation and encouragement.

One winter afternoon in 1904, Sunyer met the striking Fernande Olivier as he headed to the house of a mutual friend, the Catalan Moderniste painter Ricard Canals. Fernande was working as a model and was already being courted by Pablo Picasso, albeit rather unsuccessfully. She decided to have dinner with Sunyer and later wrote in her journal, "He's quite young and has a strong face...He's very well dressed, quite elegant even." When they became lovers and moved in together, Fernande noted with a sigh, "His studio is depressing and he has no money." There were rumors, however, that Sunyer had wealthy mistresses who provided him with "everything he needs except money." Fernande found it suspicious when he arrived home one day with "a package that contained underclothes for himself, silk underclothes, shirts, underpants and socks."

The day she decided to part ways with Sunyer, Fernande crossed paths with Picasso once again. She recalled the Spanish artist's frenzy: "With his comical accent he said, 'Biens, biens' for 'Viens' [come to my place] 'I love you, I shall do everything for you—you don't know what I could do.'"

Picasso and Fernande's seven-year relationship began on a rather hallucinatory note. As she revealed in her diary, "It's probably thanks to opium that I've discovered the true meaning of the word 'love'...I've discovered that at last I understand Pablo, I 'sense' him better." Mischievously, she also confessed, "I no longer think of getting up in the middle of the night and going off to find Sunyer, as I was still doing only recently..."

As for Sunyer, he eventually turned his back on the debauchery of the bohemian lifestyle in Paris and moved back to Sitges permanently in 1911. By then the village's famous Moderniste festivals had been replaced by a more conservative movement called Noucentisme ["1900-isms"]. While the Moderniste movement had turned toward European cultures for inspiration, Noucentiste supporters wanted to bring the focus back to Catalonia, toward the Mediterranean "as the origin of the classic culture." Sunyer took the lead and chose to emphasize local art based on "timeless values, such as the Mediterranean tradition, the Latin world, classicism, clarity and craft."

Noucentisme gained popularity in Catalonia in 1911 when the Catalan writer Eugeni d'Ors, who coined the movement's name, published a manifesto, *L'almanach dels Noucentistes*. Echoing the political and social situation in Catalonia at the time, Noucentiste painters were fighting for a return to harmony and order on the canvas. Sunyer's most famous painting, *Mediterranean Sitges*, is considered "a paradigm of *noucentista* Catalan painting." The idyllic landscape showcases the sea, the *lamporo* fishing boats, the cliffs around the bay, and the lush vegetation. As Sunyer explained, "A work of art must be of candid and pure simplicity. Art must follow tradition. And should cause no surprise or great upheaval." Like all art movements, Noucentisme reflected the needs and desires of young artists at the time and marked a necessary change, however impermanent. Joaquim Sunyer, Sitges's beloved painter, is buried in the cemetery of Saint Sebastià, in

The Palace Mar-i-cel
(*©Jean-Pierre Raguenaud*)

the fisherman's quarter. His grave is often brightened by fresh flowers.

In March 1928, Sitges was once again at the center of an artistic revolution. Salvador Dalí, who was on the brink of international stardom, traveled to the vibrant village to issue his *Manifest Groc* (Yellow manifesto), which he had written with the art critics Lluís Montanyà and Sebastià Gasch. Dalí's paintings had been rejected by the Salon d'Automne because of their "erotic allusions." In his determination to turn "each obstacle obstinately into an opportunity to go forward," Dalí published the manifesto as a rebuttal—"as insulting as a slap"—to the official judges in Paris. He then went on to paint ever more scandalous paintings, "[e]ver forward, ever stronger. Ever more Dalinian."

The influential avant-garde journal *L'Amiç de les Arts*, published in Sitges, announced Dalí's visit. Its readership was eager to see one of its regular contributors take center stage to fight the official Salon. Dalí argued that, like an old shoe, "[o]nce art gets too old and drab for our sensibility to be of any use, it should be put away. It becomes history."

Reading from his *Manifest Groc* in front of like-minded artists in Sitges's town hall, "in the mocking and quite shrill manner of his later public appearances," Dalí declared, "We denounce the absolute lack of decision and audacity...We denounce the fear of new realities, of words, of the risk of ridicule...We denounce the lethargy of the putrefied atmosphere of the circles and egos having to do with art...We denounce the young people who seek to repeat ancient painting...We denounce the painters of twisted trees" (such as

Cézanne). After a passionate list of denunciations mocking imitators and traditionalists, the artist proceeded to name "the great artists of today representing the most diverse tendencies and categories," including Picasso, Juan Gris, Joan Miró, and most of his fellow Surrealist poets and painters.

The great pioneers of modern art would have agreed with Dalí when he concluded that "art that is of use for us today, and that suits us, is beyond a doubt the one designated as art of the avant-garde, that is to say, the new art. The art of the past...was, you may rest assured, new in its own time; like the art of today, it was made up in accordance with the norms of its time, and therefore, in accordance with the people who had to use it."

From the mountain village of Horta de Sant Joan to the bustling *rambla* of Figueres, from the quaint promenade along the harbor of Banyuls-sur-Mer to the new exhibits at the renowned art museum in Céret, French and Spanish Catalonia keep surprising and enchanting visitors. The extraordinary cultural heritage of these seventeen villages can leave us breathless as we try to innumerate the long list of artists who found joy, inspiration, and encouragement here to better define themselves and their art. They discovered the Mediterranean light, the unpredictable rocky coast, and the dignity of the Canigou Mountain as it guards all the surrounding villages. Most importantly, they forged friendships with Catalan artists who guided them toward their most authentic selves. Forever linked to three major art movements—Fauvism, Cubism, and Surrealism—Catalonia can now be recognized for the critical role it played in the development of modern art.

BIOGRAPHIES

Bausil, Louis (1876–1945)

Bausil was born in Perpignan, French Catalonia. Recognized as an Impressionist painter, Bausil often painted Catalonia's bright peach, apple, and cherry blossoms in the spring. He developed a close friendship with the painter George-Daniel de Monfreid, who finished two well-received portraits of Bausil. As a member of the Artistes Roussillonnais, Bausil exhibited in Perpignan with de Monfreid and his fellow Catalan artists Aristide Maillol, Étienne Terrus, and Gustave Violet.

Braque, Georges (1882–1963)

Braque began his career as a house painter, continuing in the footsteps of his father and grandfather. When he turned to painting, he was first associated with the Fauvist movement, exhibiting with the "Wild Beasts" at the 1905 Salon d'Automne in Paris. He then cocreated Cubism with Pablo Picasso, developing Analytic and then Synthetic Cubism between 1908 and 1914. When World War I began, Braque was called to the front, where he suffered severe head injuries. He eventually returned to painting, sculpting, and producing book illustrations and lithographs.

Buñuel, Luis (1900–1983)

Buñuel was an award-winning Spanish filmmaker. While attending the University of Madrid, he became close friends with Salvador Dalí and Federico García Lorca. In 1928, with the collaboration of his friends, Buñuel directed one of the first Surrealist films, titled *Un chien andalou*. Throughout his life he directed and produced politically driven films, often attacking bourgeois values and denouncing the clergy. In 1961, his film *Viridiana* won the Palme d'Or at the Cannes Film Festival. In 1947, he relocated permanently to Mexico City with his wife and children.

Casagemas, Carles (1880–1901)

Casagemas was a Spanish painter who became Pablo Picasso's closest friend during the men's early twenties. The two friends discovered Paris together for the first time in 1900 during the World Fair. Tragically, Casagemas fell in love with an artist's model named Germaine (who would later marry the Catalan painter Ramón Pitxot). When she refused his advances, he shot at her in a crowded restaurant, missed, and then turned the gun on himself. Picasso began his Blue Period when he buried his best friend.

Casals, Pau (1876–1973)

Casals was born in El Vendrell, Spanish Catalonia. Recognized as one of the most gifted cellists in the world, Casals was forced to go into exile during the Spanish Civil War, settling in Prades, French Catalonia. In 1950, he agreed to play in public again and head the Prades Music Festival in honor of Johann Sebastian Bach. The festival still takes places every summer, attracting international musicians and visitors with its chamber music concerts in the town's Church of Saint Pierre and in the nearby abbey of Saint Michel de Cuxa. At age ninety-three, Casals was asked why he still practiced the cello every day, to which he replied, "I think I'm getting better."

Casas, Ramon (1866–1932)

Born in Barcelona, Casas came from a well-to-do family that had made a fortune in Cuba. Casas became a well-known illustrator for several magazines, a graphic designer of postcards and posters, as well as a Moderniste painter who exhibited throughout France, Spain, Germany, and the U.S. In 1889, he illustrated a book with his friend Santiago Rusiñol titled *Per Catalunya (des del meu carro)* after a road trip through the region. In 1897, he opened Els Quatre Gats in Barcelona with his friends Rusiñol the painter, art critic Miquel Utrillo, and Pere Romeu.

Chagall, Marc (1887–1985)

Born in Belarus, Chagall moved to Paris in 1910. As he exhibited at the Salon des Indépendants and the Salon d'Automne, the painter developed close friendships with avant-garde artists like the poet Max Jacob and painters Chaïm Soutine, Pinchus Kremegne, and Moise Kisling. Chagall traveled twice to Céret, French Catalonia, to enjoy the sunny climate and inexpensive accommodations. Chagall also lived in Tossa de Mar in Spanish Catalonia during the summer of 1934.

Dalí, Salvador (1904–1989)

Dalí was born in Figueres, Spanish Catalonia, where his father worked as a notary. The family also owned a summer home in nearby Cadaqués. At the age of twenty-two, Dalí fell in love with Gala, the wife of poet Paul Éluard and the woman who would become Dalí's lifelong muse. They built a home together in Port Lligat with a studio overlooking the Mediterranean Sea. Dalí is recognized as the greatest Surrealist painter. In addition to painting, he designed the Teatro-Museu in Figueres, which is today the most visited site in Spanish Catalonia.

De Monfreid, George-Daniel (1856–1929)

De Monfreid was a French painter who lived part of each year in Corneilla-de-Conflent, French Catalonia. As an artist and a generous friend, de Monfreid opened his home, le Château de Saint Clément, to Henri Matisse, Aristide Maillol, Étienne Terrus, Louis Bausil, Gustave Fayet, and many others. He became one of the leading supporters of Paul Gauguin's work. He often displayed Gauguin's paintings in his studio, moving his own artwork to the back of the room. De Monfreid is the father of the celebrated travel writer Henry de Monfreid.

De Monfreid, Henry (1879–1974)

A French explorer and the author of over seventy books, de Monfreid spent some of his childhood summers in Corneilla-de-Conflent, French Catalonia. In 1911, he moved to Djibouti with his second wife, Armgart Freudenfeld. They had three children together, Gisèle, Amélie, and Daniel. His most famous autobiographical work is titled *Secrets of the Red Sea*.

De Séverac, Déodat (1872–1921)

De Séverac was a French composer best known for his suite Cerdaña and his critically acclaimed opera *Héliogabale*. In early 1910, he moved to Céret, French Catalonia, where he joined his friends Frank Burty Haviland and Manolo Hugué. He developed close friendships with Catalan artists Étienne Terrus, Gustave Violet, Aristide Maillol, and George-Daniel de Monfreid. He died in Céret at the age of forty eight.

Derain, André (1880–1954)

The French painter developed the Fauvist art movement along with Henri Matisse during the summer of 1905 in Collioure,

French Catalonia. He then turned to Cubism and became friends with Pablo Picasso and other Cubist painters. In the summer of 1910, he traveled to Cadaqués, Spanish Catalonia, to visit Picasso and Ramón Pitxot. Later in life, Derain worked as a designer on book illustrations and stage sets.

Dufy, Raoul (1877–1953)

Dufy was first a Fauvist painter and was largely influenced by Henri Matisse's work. By the 1920s, however, Dufy developed his own personal style of painting and focused on cheerful depictions of life by the Mediterranean Sea. His favorite themes included regatta races, orchestras, and beach scenes. He is best known for his over-6,000-square-foot painting *La fée éléctricité*, which was exhibited in Paris in 1937 at the International Exhibition of Art and Technology.

Éluard, Paul (1895–1952)

The French poet was one of the founders of the Surrealist movement in Paris, alongside his friends Louis Aragon and André Breton. In 1917, he married Gala, with whom he had a daughter named Cecile. Together they traveled to Cadaqués, Spanish Catalonia, to visit Salvador Dalí. Gala subsequently divorced him to be with Dalí. Over the course of his career, Éluard published more than seventy literary and political works, including poems dedicated to his friends Max Ernst and Pablo Picasso, the latter of whom was present at his funeral.

Ernst, Max (1891–1976)

Well-known in the Dada movement, Ernst was a German-born artist who experimented with photomontages, collages, painting, and sculpting. From 1921 through 1924, he developed a close relationship with the poet Paul Éluard and his wife, Gala. With Éluard, André Breton, Louis Aragon, and others, Ernst helped found the Surrealist movement in Paris, initiating new techniques including frottage (pencil rubbing of objects) and decalcomania (pressing paint by folding the paper in half). After World War II, he lived in the U.S. and married the gallery owner Peggy Guggenheim. He later married the painter Dorothea Tanning and moved back to France, traveling to Collioure, French Catalonia, in the 1950s.

Fayet, Gustave (1865–1925)

Fayet was born in Béziers to a wealthy family of viticulturists and landowners. He built one of the most exciting art collections of the twentieth century, showcasing works by Gauguin, Odilon Redon, Matisse, Degas, Cézanne, and many others. In 1908, Fayet purchased the Abbey of Fontfroide near Narbonne and spent years renovating it to its full glory. Fayet was also an accomplished ceramicist, painter, and book illustrator. In the 1920s, he opened a tapestry workshop with his friend Fernand Dumas. They used his watercolors to design extraordinary rugs that were exhibited at the Salon d'Automne and the Pavillon Marsan in Paris to critical acclaim.

Gauguin, Paul (1848–1903)

Before he committed to painting as a career, Gauguin traveled to Cerbère, French Catalonia, in 1883 to help exiled Spanish revolutionaries fight the government. As a painter, Gauguin first embraced Impressionism but by the late 1880s had developed a more distinct style as he led the Symbolist art movement. He moved to Tahiti in 1893, and then to Atuona in the Marquesas Islands, where he is buried. Considered a leader in modern art, Gauguin influenced countless artists, including Henri Matisse, Pablo Picasso, and Aristide Maillol.

Gris, Juan (1887–1927)

Gris was a Spanish Cubist painter who lived in the Bateau-Lavoir studios in Paris. After forging a friendship with Pablo Picasso, he traveled to Céret, French Catalonia, to join the Cubist master in 1913. He returned in 1921 during the winter months. Gris also designed sets for the famous Russian Ballet company. He died at the age of forty.

Hanicotte, Augustin (1870–1957)

The French painter met Aristide Maillol in Banyuls-sur-Mer in 1915. The sculptor encouraged him to visit Collioure, where he stayed for over twenty years. In 1925, Hanicotte founded a children's art program in the elementary school called Les Gosses de Collioure. He took students around the village, sometimes to the same spots where Matisse and Derain painted in 1905, and organized art exhibits of the children's work throughout France.

Haviland, Frank Burty (1878–1972)

Haviland was born in Limoges, France, where his American father owned a successful porcelain business. Through his interest in the arts, Haviland befriended the Spanish Catalan composer Ricardo Viñes, who became his piano teacher. He also developed close friendships with the French composer Déodat de Séverac and the Catalan sculptor Manolo Hugué. Together they moved to Céret in French Catalonia in 1909. Haviland purchased and renovated an old monastery, Le Couvent des Capucins, where he lived with his wife, Joséphine Laporta. It became a gathering place for visiting artists, including Pablo Picasso. In 1956, Haviland became curator of the Musée d'Art Moderne in Céret. The artist has been immortalized by his friends in several sculptures and paintings, including Juan Gris's *The Smoker* and Amedeo Modigliani's *Portrait of Frank Burty Haviland*. Haviland died in Céret at the age of ninety-four.

Hemingway, Ernest (1899–1961)

Hemingway lived in Paris in the 1920s, working as a journalist for the *Toronto Star* newspaper. His first success as a writer came in 1926 when he published *The Sun Also Rises*. He befriended the Surrealist painter Joan Miró, who invited him to Mont-Roig del Camp, in Spanish Catalonia. Hemingway had a deep passion for Catalonia and Spain, which serve as a background for several of his short stories and novels, including his masterpiece *For Whom the Bell Tolls*. Hemingway won the Nobel Prize for Literature in 1954.

Herbin, Auguste (1882–1960)

The French Cubist painter Herbin kept a studio in the Bateau-Lavoir complex, adjacent to Picasso's apartment. He joined the Cubist master in Céret, French Catalonia, in 1913. After World War II, he lived in Céret from 1918 until 1920 and returned once more in 1923.

Horszowski, Mieczyslaw (1892–1993)

Born in Poland, Horszowski became a piano prodigy, playing in public at the age of eight. He met the cellist Pau Casals in his teen years, and the two became lifelong friends. He traveled to Prades, French Catalonia, many times to participate in the Music Festival alongside Casals. George-Daniel de Monfreid's daughter, Agnès, opened her home in Corneilla-de-Conflent to the pianist during his summer visits. Horszowski is believed to be the first pianist to record while playing the oldest known piano, which dates from 1720 and was built by Bartolomeo Cristofori.

Hugué, Manolo (1872–1945)

Born in Barcelona, the Catalan sculptor moved to Céret, French Catalonia, in 1909, where he lived until 1927. His presence in Céret attracted many artists living in Paris in the 1910s and '20s. He had a charming personality and grew close to Frank Burty Haviland, Déodat de Séverac, Pablo Picasso, Georges Braque, Étienne Terrus, Aristide Maillol, and many others. There are several of Manolo's sculptures on display in the village and in the Musée d'Art Moderne.

Jacob, Max (1876–1944)

The French poet became close friends with Pablo Picasso and many other artists who lived in the Bateau Lavoir studios in Paris. Jacob coined the studios' name because the place reminded him of the laundry boats found along the Seine River. Jacob traveled to Céret, French Catalonia, in 1913 to visit Picasso. He wrote the novel *Saint Matorel* and the collections *Le laboratoire central* and *La défense de Tartuffe*.

Kahnweiler, Daniel-Henry (1884–1974)

Born in Germany, Kahnweiler moved to Paris in 1907 and became a leading art collector and dealer during the twentieth century. He offered contracts to Manolo Hugué, André Derain, Pablo Picasso, Georges Braque, Juan Gris, and others when they were struggling financially. Later in life, Kahnweiler became a writer, publishing articles and books, including *Der Weg zum Kubismus* on the development of Cubism.

Kipling, Rudyard (1865–1936)

Kipling was only forty two years old when he received the Nobel Prize for Literature in 1907. Born in India and raised in England, the prolific writer is well known for his novel *The Jungle Book*, his travel writing, his short stories, and his children's books. In 1910, 1911, and 1914, Kipling and his wife visited Vernet-les-Bains, in French Catalonia, to enjoy the benefits of the famous health resort.

Kisling, Moise (1891–1953)

Kisling was a Polish painter. He moved to Paris and became friends with many avant-garde artists, including Chaïm Soutine, Pinchus Kremegne, and Amedeo Modigliani. In 1912 and 1913, he lived in Céret, French Catalonia, where he painted many landscapes. However, he is mostly remembered for his ephemeral female nudes and portraits.

Lorca Federico, García (1898–1936)

Lorca was a renowned Spanish poet and playwright. He attended the University of Madrid, where he met Salvador Dalí and became one of his closest friends. He visited Dalí in Cadaqués as he worked on his poetry collection. He was shot and killed at the age of thirty-eight by supporters of General Franco during the Spanish Civil War.

Machado, Antonio (1875–1939)

The celebrated Spanish poet published several collections, including *Soledades*, *Campos de Castilla*, and *Nuevas Canciones*. When the Spanish Civil War broke out, Machado went into exile in Collioure, French Catalonia. He is buried in the local cemetery.

Mackintosh, Charles Rennie (1868–1928)

The Scottish architect was a leader in the Arts and Crafts movement. He met his wife, the artist Margaret MacDonald, at the Glasgow School of Art. Mackintosh designed furniture, textiles and home interiors. Toward the end of his life, Mackintosh moved to Port-Vendres, French Catalonia, where he perfected his skills as a painter.

Maillol, Aristide (1861–1944)

Maillol was born in Banyuls-sur-Mer, French Catalonia. He began his career as a painter and tapestry designer but soon turned to sculpting. His friend George-Daniel de Monfreid, who lived in nearby Corneilla, supported him during his most poverty-stricken years. In 1905, Maillol exhibited *La Méditerranée* to critical acclaim, an accomplishment that brought him important commissions and led to international success. He divided his time between Paris and Banyuls-sur-Mer, where he owned a farmhouse, which is now open to the public.

Manguin, Henri (1874–1949)

While attending the École des Beaux-Arts, the French painter befriended Albert Marquet and Henri Matisse. Manguin played an important role in the Fauvist movement, which began at the 1905 Salon d'Automne. One of the earliest avant-garde paintings in the Gertrude and Leo Stein collection was Manguin's 1904 *L'atelier, le model nu.* In the summer of 1906, Manguin traveled to Collioure, French Catalonia, to join Matisse for three weeks.

Marquet, Albert (1875–1947)

The French painter became close friends with Henri Matisse at the École des Beaux Arts in Paris during the 1890s. He embraced Fauvism, exhibiting his work at the 1905 Salon d'Automne. Marquet first saw the Mediterranean Sea as a boy on a family vacation. One of his earliest memories was approaching the sea in awe of its turquoise color, only to be disappointed when he cupped some of the water in his hands and the color disappeared. Throughout his life, Marquet traveled extensively and lived in Algiers from 1940 until 1945.

Marre, Henri (1858–1927)

A French Pointillist painter, Marre traveled to Collioure in 1910, where he lived and worked until his death in 1927.

Matisse, Henri (1869–1954)

Matisse was born in the north of France. He attended the École des Beaux-Arts in Paris, where he befriended the painters Albert Marquet and Henri Manguin. In the summer of 1905, he traveled to Collioure, French Catalonia, where he developed Fauvism with the painter André Derain. His early supporters included the Stein family, the Russian art collector Sergei Shchukin, and the Cone sisters, Clarabel and Etta, in Baltimore, Maryland. After discovering Catalonia, Matisse continued to travel. He spent time in Italy, Corsica, Algeria, Morocco, the United States, and Tahiti. In his later years, living in Nice, Matisse completed beautiful large-scale paper cut-outs, which he called "painting with scissors." His last project consisted of designing and decorating the interior and the glass windows of the Chapelle du Rosaire in Vence.

Miró, Joan (1893–1983)

The Spanish Catalan artist divided his time between Mont-Roig del Camp in Catalonia and Paris. He joined the Surrealist movement in 1924. In addition to paintings, Miró also created ceramics, tapestries, and large sculptures, many of which are on display in European museums and in the United States.

Mucha, Willy (1905–1995)

The Polish painter relocated to Collioure, French Catalonia, in 1940 and lived on the Côte Vermeille for most of his life. He kept a *livre d'or*, which has signatures from over ninety artists whom he met in Collioure and throughout his travels, including Raoul Dufy, Pablo Picasso, Georges Braque, Marc Chagall, Salvador Dalí, and Max Ernst. The large blue mosaic panel on the façade of the hotel Les Templiers is based on a drawing by Mucha.

O'Brian, Patrick (1914–2000)

The British writer was born Richard Patrick Russ. The author of *Master and Commander* finished twenty novels in his well-known Aubrey-Maturin nautical series. In 1949, O'Brian moved to Collioure, French Catalonia, with his second wife, Mary Tolstoy. In addition to writing, O'Brian also translated French works into English and wrote a biography on Pablo Picasso. He died in Dublin in 2000 but is buried in Collioure next to his wife, who passed away in 1998.

Picasso, Pablo (1881–1973)

Picasso moved to Catalonia at age thirteen and enjoyed returning to the region as an adult. One of the most prolific painters in the world, Picasso redefined his style throughout his career. After his Blue Period and his Pink Period, he codeveloped Cubism with his friend Georges Braque. The two artists spent several weeks together in the summer of 1911 in Céret, French Catalonia. Picasso returned in 1912 and 1913. His painting *Les demoiselles d'Avignon* signaled the beginning of Cubism. It represents prostitutes in a Barcelona brothel on Avignon Street, not in the French town of Avignon, as is sometimes mistakenly described. During the Spanish Civil War, Picasso completed *Guernica*, another masterpiece, which depicts the horrors of the war. It was presented at the World Fair in Paris in 1937 and is now on display at the Museo Reina Sofia in Madrid.

Pitxot, Ramón (1872–1925)

The Catalan Impressionist painter kept a home in Cadaqués, Spanish Catalonia. He was an early influence on Salvador Dalí, who was a close family friend. Pitxot also developed a friendship with Pablo Picasso, who visited him in Cadaqués in the summer of 1910. His wife, Germaine, had been a model and the mistress of the Cubist master in the early 1900s. According to Picasso's biographer, John Richardson, when Picasso learned of Pitxot's sudden death at the age of fifty-three, he added his friend into the painting he was working on at the time, titled *Three Dancers*.

Redon, Odilon (1840–1916)

The French Symbolist painter and graphic designer first worked in charcoal and lithography, which he used to produce his famous series *Les noirs*. In 1889, he exhibited with Paul Gauguin at *Les XX* in Brussels. They shared mutual friends in the avant-garde Nabis group, including Pierre Bonnard and Paul Serusier. The two artists kept up a correspondence until Gauguin's death in 1903. In 1899, Redon switched to colorful pastels and oils. In 1910–1911, he traveled several times to the art collector Gustave Fayet's Abbey of Fontfroide in the south of France. Fayet commissioned his friend to paint two large wall panels, titled *Le jour* and *La nuit*, and a smaller one above the door, titled *Silence*, for his personal library.

Rusiñol, Santiago (1861–1931)

Born in Barcelona, Rusiñol moved to Paris to study painting. He returned to Catalonia and headed the Modernisme movement from Sitges, where he purchased a home and studio in 1892. He had close ties with other Catalan artists, including Ramon Casas and Miquel Utrillo, who helped him organize the famous Moderniste festivals in Sitges. In addition to being a painter, Rusiñol was also a talented poet and playwright.

Schneider, Alexander (1908–1993)

Born in Lithuania, Schneider became a violinist and eventually joined the Budapest Quartet in the early 1930s. While the orchestra was on tour in the United States, World War II began, and the musicians were allowed to stay in the country permanently. In 1950, Schneider organized the first Prades music festival, which commemorated the 200th anniversary of Johann Sebastian Bach's death. Today, the annual Casals Festival still brings international musicians together to perform for three weeks each summer in Prades, French Catalonia. From 1957 until his death in 1993, Schneider was the artistic director of the Schneider Concerts at the New School in New York.

Signac, Paul (1863–1935)

The French painter led the Pointillist art movement after the death of Georges Seurat in 1891. In 1899, he published an important work about the movement titled *From Eugene Delacroix to Neo-Impressionism*. He was an early supporter of Henri Matisse and encouraged him to discover the landscape and the extraordinary light of the Mediterranean region. Signac traveled to Collioure in the late 1880s, but he preferred to spend time in Saint Tropez, where he kept a home.

Soutine, Chaïm (1893–1943)

Soutine had a difficult childhood and continued to struggle physically and emotionally as he endured debilitating poverty throughout his life. Fellow exiled painters from Eastern Europe like Pinchus Kremegne, Marc Chagall, and Moise Kisling befriended him when he moved to Paris in 1913. He developed a close friendship with Amedeo Modigliani, who introduced him to an art collector named Leopold Sborowski. In 1919, Soutine moved to Céret, French Catalonia, where he painted over 300 works. The Expressionist painter reached international renown and financial security when the American collector Dr. Albert Barnes became his *mécène*, or patron.

Stein, Gertrude (1874–1946)

Stein was an American writer who moved to Paris in 1903 and remained there for the rest of her life. With her brother Leo, she began collecting the artworks of Paul Cézanne, Henri Manguin, Henri Matisse, and Pablo Picasso, long before the critics and the general public realized their importance. Matisse and Picasso were introduced to one another at Stein's legendary weekly salon in her home on Rue de Fleurus. She became a close friend to both artists and often offered her opinion and advice, which they respected greatly. Stein is the author of, among others, *Three Lives*, *Tender Buttons*, and *The Autobiography of Alice B. Toklas*. Leo and Gertrude Stein's brother Michael and his wife, Sarah, were also influential collectors with a penchant for Matisse's work.

Sunyer, Joaquim (1874–1956)

Sunyer was born in Sitges, Spanish Catalonia. He studied painting in Paris, where he lived for several years in the famous Bateau Lavoir complex. He befriended many Post-Impressionist and Cubist artists, including Pablo Picasso. The two met again when they both lived in Céret, French Catalonia, in the early 1910s. Sunyer eventually took the lead in the Noucentisme art movement in Catalonia with his celebrated painting *Pastoral*. He is buried in Sitges.

55

Survage, Leopold (1879–1968)

Born in Finland, Survage arrived in Paris in 1909, where he enrolled in Henri Matisse's newly established painting academy. Beginning in 1925, he traveled to Collioure, French Catalonia, for the summer months, staying at the Quintana hotel. He followed the Cubist movement but also developed a talent in tapestry and textile and stage designs. Several of his paintings are now part of the permanent exhibition at the Musée d'Art Moderne of Céret.

Terrus, Étienne (1857–1922)

Terrus was born in Elne, French Catalonia. Fiercely loyal to Catalonia and unimpressed by the artistic trends in Paris, Terrus proved to be an important influence on Henri Matisse. They developed a close friendship that lasted until 1917, the year Matisse sent his last, thirteen-page-long letter, which has since mysteriously disappeared. In addition to being a talented watercolor artist, Terrus was also an avid photographer. His home in Elne, where he lived with his wife, is still standing today as private property. Visitors can pay homage to the artist by visiting the Terrus Museum, which stands adjacent to the Cathedral of Saint Eulalie and Saint Julie and its Romanesque cloister.

Utrillo, Miquel (1862–1934)

The Catalan painter managed the legendary bar Els Quatre Gats in Barcelona with his fellow artists Ramon Casas and Santiago Rusiñol. The Modernista painters supported the early careers of several Spanish artists, including Pablo Picasso, who held his first exhibition at Els Quatre Gats in 1900. The multitalented Utrillo became a well-known art critic, architect, and designer. Although he was not the biological father of the painter Maurice Utrillo, he recognized the child as his own to help his friend the model and painter Suzanne Valadon.

Valtat, Louis (1869–1952)

An early proponent of bright colors and decorative elements in artwork, Valtat influenced Henri Matisse and the Fauvist movement. He traveled to Catalonia for health reasons, and became friends with Aristide Maillol and George-Daniel de Monfreid. Like many artists in the Nabis group, Valtat was influenced by Paul Gauguin's work. He also befriended Pierre-Auguste Renoir, who painted a portrait of the artist as well as one of his wife, Suzanne Valtat.

Viñes, Ricardo (1875–1943)

Viñes was born in Lleida, Spanish Catalonia. He became a well-known pianist who befriended Maurice Ravel, Déodat de Séverac, Claude Debussy, and Erik Satie, whose compositions he often performed in France and Spain. Beginning in 1908, he often visited his friend Gustave Fayet at the Abbey of Fontfroide and spent time with fellow artists including the painter Odilon Redon. The twenty-five recordings he left behind are available today from Marston Records. His hometown hosts an international piano competition each year in Viñes's honor.

Violet, Gustave (1873–1952)

A strong advocate for the arts in Catalonia, Violet developed a successful career as a sculptor, an architect, a playwright, and a translator of Catalan writings. With a studio set up in Prades, in French Catalonia, Violet completed a bust of his friend George-Daniel de Monfreid, as well as several monuments around Catalonia, including the *Entente cordiale* monument in Vernet-les-Bains. Violet belonged to the Catalan group Les Artistes Roussillonnais. Together, the artists of the group exhibited their work in Perpignan to an enthusiastic public and press. "[Violet] dreams with his hands," wrote one critic.

Vollard, Ambroise (1866–1939)

Vollard was one of the leading art collectors and dealers in Paris. He sold the works of André Derain, Aristide Maillol, Louis Valtat, Paul Gauguin, Pablo Picasso, and many others. He also worked with Marc Chagall on a series of lithographs to illustrate the French fables of Jean de La Fontaine. Vollard was also an editor and writer and published a biography titled *En écoutant Cézanne, Degas, Renoir.*

BIBLIOGRAPHY

Chapter One

Barou, Jean-Pierre. *Collioure 1905, Matisse fauve.* Perpignan, France: Éditions Mare Nostrum, 2005.

Barou, Jean-Pierre. *Matisse ou le miracle de Collioure.* Montpellier, France: Indigène Éditions, 1997.

Bernadi, François. *Matisse et Derain: À Collioure, été 1905.* Collioure, France: Éditions Les Amis du Musée de Collioure, 1989.

Deloncle Saint-Ramon, Catherine. *1905–1954: Les pionniers de l'art moderne en pays Catalan.* Amélie-les-Bains, France: Alter Ego Éditions, 2005.

Exhibition catalogue. Salle Maillol au Palais des Congrès, Perpignan du 4 Juillet au 27 Septembre 1998. *1894–1908: Le Roussillon à l'origine de l'art moderne.* Montpellier, France: Indigène Éditions, 1998.

King, Dean. *Patrick O'Brian: A Life.* New York, NY: Henry Holt and Company, 2001.

Grammont, Claudine, ed. *Matisse-Marquet: Correspondance 1898–1947.* Lausanne, Switzerland: La Bibliothèque des Arts, 2008.

Mucha, Willy. *L'esprit du clocher.* Caixas, France: Collection Willy Mucha, Fondation de Collioure, 1981.

Musée d'Art Moderne de Céret. Exposition du 18 Juin au 2 Octobre, 2005. *Matisse-Derain: Collioure 1905, un été fauve.* Paris, France: Éditions Gallimard, 2005.

Musée Terrus. Exposition du 27 Juin au 30 Septembre, 2009. *Henri Manguin: Fauve et précurseur (1898–1906).* Montpellier, France: Indigène Editions, 2009.

Spurling, Hilary. *The Unknown Matisse.* New York, NY: Random House, 2005.

Tolstoy, Nikolai. *Patrick O'Brian: The Making of the Novelist*. London, England: Century Books, 2004.

Chapter Two

Bonnel, Jean-Pierre, and André Roger. *Dina Vierny: Une grande dame au pays de Maillol*. Villelongue-de-la-Salanque, France: Éditions Frontières, 2000.

Cahn, Isabelle, Jean-Luc Daval, and Bertrand Lorquin, eds. *L'ABCdaire de Maillol*. Paris, France: Éditions Flammarion, 1996.

Crichton, Robin. *Monsieur Mackintosh*. Edinburgh, Scotland: Luath Press Limited, 2006.

Deloncle Saint-Ramon, Catherine. *1905–1954: Les pionniers de l'art moderne en pays Catalan*. Amélie-les-Bains, France: Alter Ego Éditions, 2005.

Fayol, Armelle. "Louis Valtat, à l'aube du fauvisme." *Dossiers de l'art*, no. 186: 2–35.

Gauguin, Paul. *Correspondence. Selections de Paul Gauguin*. Paris, France: Fondation Singer-Polignac, 1984.

Grimes, William. "Dina Vierny, Artist's Muse, Dies at 89." *New York Times*, January 27, 2009.

Kostenevich, Albert. *French Art Treasures at the Hermitage: Splendid Masterpieces, New Discoveries*. New York, NY: Harry N. Abrams, Inc., Publishers, 1999.

Philip, R., and Paul Gauguin. *The Early Work of Paul Gauguin: Genesis of an Artist*. Cincinnati, OH: Cincinnati Art Museum, 1971.

Valaison, Marie-Claude. "Maillol et le Roussillon." *Terres Catalanes* (1994): 49–54.

Vollard, Ambroise. *Recollections of a Picture Dealer*. Translated from the French by Violet M. MacDonald. Mineola, NY: Dover Publications, Inc., 2002.

Wise, Susan. *Paul Gauguin: His Life and His Paintings*. Chicago, IL: The Art Institute of Chicago, 1980.

Shackelford, George T.M., and Claire Frèches-Thory. *Gauguin Tahiti*. Boston, MA: Museum of Fine Arts, 2004.

Chapter Three

De Monfreid, George-Daniel. The unpublished personal journals, 1896–1929. Owned by Marc Latham, the painter's great-grandson.

De Monfreid, George-Daniel. *Sur Paul Gauguin*. La Rochelle, France: Éditions Rumeur des Ages, 2003.

Exhibition catalogue. *Collection G.D. de Monfreid du 25 avril au 27 mai 1951*. Paris, France: Musée National d'Art Moderne, 1951.

Gauguin, Paul. *The Letters of Paul Gauguin to Georges Daniel de Monfreid*. Translated from the French by Ruth Pielkovo. New York, NY: Dodd, Mead and Company, Inc., 1922.

Gauguin, Paul. *Avant et après*. Paris, France: Collection la Petite Vermillon. Les Éditions de la Table Ronde. 1994.

Gauguin, Pola. *My Father, Paul Gauguin*. Translated by Arthur G. Chater. New York, NY: Alfred A. Knopf Publisher, 1937.

Loize, Jean. *Les amitiés du peintre Georges-Daniel de Monfreid et ses reliques de Gauguin: de Maillol et Codet à Ségalen*. Paris, France: Chez Jean Loize, 1951.

Malingue, Maurice, ed. *Paul Gauguin: Lettres à sa femme et à ses amis*. Paris, France: Les Cahiers Rouges, Éditions Grasset, 1946.

Pagé, Georges. *Henry de Monfreid: L'aventurier de la mer Rouge*. Paris, France: Éditions Grancher, 2008.

Shackelford, George T.M., and Claire Frèches-Thory. *Gauguin Tahiti*. Boston, MA: Museum of Fine Arts, 2004.

Walther, Ingo F. *Gauguin*. Cologne, Germany: Taschen Editions, 1996.

Chapter Four

Clavell, Xavier Costa. *Picasso: Musée Picasso de Barcelone*. Barcelona, Spain: Editorial Fisa Escudo de Oro, 1982.

Deloncle, Catherine. *Une érection salvatrice en gare de Perpignan: Centre de l'univers*. Céret, France: Alter Ego Éditions, 2006.

Kahnweiler, Daniel-Henry. *My Galleries and Painters*. Translated from the French by Helen Weaver. Boston, MA: Museum of Fine Arts Publications, 2003.

Matamoros, Joséphine, ed. *Guide to the Collections of the Museum of Modern Art in Céret*. Céret, France: Éditions Les Amis du Musée d'Art Moderne de Céret, 1999.

Olivier, Fernande. *Loving Picasso: The Private Journal of Fernande Olivier*. Translated from the French by Christine Baker and Michael Raeburn. New York, NY: Harry N. Abrams, Inc., Publishers, 2001.

Richardson, John. *A Life of Picasso: 1897–1906, the Painter of Modern Life*. New York, NY: Random House, Inc., 1996.

Richardson, John. *A Life of Picasso: 1907–1917, the Painter of Modern Life*. New York, NY: Random House, Inc., 1996.

Rubin, William. *Picasso and Braque: Pioneering Cubism*. New York, NY: The Museum of Modern Art, 1989.

Sabench, Étienne. *La petite histoire du Musée d'Art Moderne de Céret*. Barcelona, Spain: Editorial Mediterrània, 1994.

Zolton, Marilyn, and Raymond Zolton. *Places of Picasso: A Biographical Guide to Spain and France*. Bethlehem, NH: Raymar Associates, 1998.

Chapter Five

Barou, Jean-Pierre. *Matisse-Terrus: Histoire d'une amitié (1905–1917)*. Montpellier, France: Indigène Editions, 2002.

Collett, Sam. "Rudyard Kipling at Vernet-les-Bains." 2002. Vernet-les-Bains, Office de Tourisme. Retrieved on November 15, 2011, at http://www.vernet-dels-banys.eu/kipling/colletteng1.pdf

Exhibition catalog. Salle Maillol au Palais des Congrès, Perpignan du 4 Juillet au 27 Septembre 1998. *1894–1908: Le Roussillon à l'origine de l'art moderne*. Montpellier, France: Indigène Éditions, 1998.

Kirk, H.L. *Pablo Casals: A Biography*. New York, NY: Holt, Rinehart & Winston Publishers, 1974.

Littlehales, Lillian. *Pablo Casals*. New York, NY: Praeger Editions, 1970.

Molkhou, Jean-Michel. "Casals, un musicien d'éternité." *Diapason*, no. 582 (Juillet–Août 2010): 25–39.

Raynal, Madeleine, "Étienne Terrus (1857–1922)," *Conflent*, no. 181 (Janvier–Février 1993): 4–15.

Spurling, Hilary. *The Unknown Matisse*. New York, NY: Random House, Inc., 2005.

Vernet-les-Bains, Office de Tourisme."The Kipling Circuit." Retrieved on February 19, 2012, at http://www.vernet-les-bains.fr/vernet/iso _album/kiplingcircuit.pdf

Chapter Six

Clavell, Xavier Costa. *Picasso: Musée Picasso de Barcelone*. Barcelona, Spain: Editorial Fisa Escudo de Oro, S.A., 1982.

Mink, Janis. *Miró*. Cologne, Germany: Editions Taschen, 2006.

Olivier, Fernande. *Loving Picasso: The Private Journal of Fernande Olivier*. Translated from the French by Christine Baker and Michael Raeburn. New York, NY: Harry N. Abrams, Inc., Publishers, 2001.

Permanyer, Lluís. *Miró: The Life of a Passion*. Translated by Paul Martin. Barcelona, Spain: Edicions de 1984, 2003.

Richardson, John. *A Life of Picasso: 1881–1906, the Painter of Modern Life*. New York, NY: Random House, Inc., 1996.

Richardson, John. *A Life of Picasso: 1907–1917, the Painter of Modern Life*. New York, NY: Random House, Inc., 1996.

Stein, Gertrude. *Picasso*. New York, NY: Dover Publications, 1984.

Swinglehurst, Edmund. *The Art of the Surrealists*. Bristol, England: Parragon Book Service, 1995.

Zolton, Marilyn, and Raymond Zolton. *Places of Picasso: A Biographical Guide to Spain and France*. Bethlehem, NH: Raymar Associates, 1998.

Chapter Seven

Bellsolà, Jaume. *Cadaqués*. Barcelona, Spain: Postales Internacional, 1995.

Dalí, Salvador. *The Unspeakable Confessions of Salvador Dalí*. New York, NY: Morrow Editions, 1976.

Deloncle, Catherine: *Une érection salvatrice en gare de Perpignan: Centre de l'univers*. Céret, France: Éditions Alter Ego. 2006.

Faerna, José Maria. *Dalí*. Translated by Teresa Waldes. New York, NY: Harry N. Abrams, Inc., Publishers, 1995.

García Márquez, Gabriel. *Twelve Pilgrims: Twelve Stories*. New York, NY: Knopf Doubleday Publishing Group, 1993.

Giménez-Frontin, J.L. *Teatre-Museu Dalí*. Madrid, Spain: Editions Tusquets/Electa Art Guides, 2001.

Néret, Gilles. *Dalí*. Cologne, Germany: Editions Taschen, 2007.

Olivier, Fernande. *Loving Picasso: The Private Journal of Fernande Olivier*. Translated from the French by Christine Baker and Michael Raeburn. New York, NY: Harry N. Abrams, Inc., Publishers, 2001.

Pitxot, Antonio, and Josep Playa. *Casa-museu castell Gala Dalí: Púbol*. Barcelona, Spain: Editorial Escudo de Oro, S.A., 2000.

Pitxot, Antonio, and Montse Aguer. *Casa-museu Salvador Dalí: Port Lligat*. Barcelona, Spain: Editorial Escudo de Oro, S.A., 2002.

Richardson, John. *A Life of Picasso: 1907–1917, the Painter of Modern Life*. New York, NY: Random House, Inc., 1996.

Chapter Eight

Alexander, Sidney. *Marc Chagall: An Intimate Biography*. Emeryville, CA: Marlow & Co., 1988.

Casacuberta, Margarida. *Rusiñol*. Barcelona, Spain: Generalitat de Catalunya, 2006.

Chagall, Marc. *My Life*. London, England: Peter Owen Publishers, 2011.

Doñate, Mercè. *Modernisme in the MNAC Collection*. Barcelona, Spain: Museu Nacional d'Art de Catalunya, 2009.

Gallagher, Mary-Ann, Nick Inman, and Roger Williams. *DK Eyewitness Travel Guide: Barcelona and Catalonia*. London, England: Dorling Kindersley Limited, 2011.

Lewis, J. Patrick, and Jane Yolen. *Self-Portrait with Seven Fingers: The Life of Marc Chagall in Verse*. Mankato, MN: Creative Editions, 2011.

Marquès, Carles. *Sitges: From White to Multicolour*. Menorca, Spain: Triangle Postals, 2009.

Richardson, John. *A Life of Picasso: 1881–1906, the Painter of Modern Life*. New York, NY: Random House, Inc., Publishers, 1996.

Wullschlüger, Jackie. *Marc Chagall: A Biography*. New York, NY: Knopf Doubleday Publishing Group, 2008.

Guidebooks

Cañagueral, Alberto, and Marie-Ange Demory. *Catalonia: French and Spanish*. Translated from the French by Y2K Translations. London, England: Hachette UK, 2001.

Bibliography

Facaros, Dana, and Michael Pauls. *Barcelona & Catalonia*. Northampton, MA: Cadogan Guides, 2010.

Hart, Maria Teresa, ed. *Barcelona: With Highlights of Catalonia & Bilbao*. New York, NY: Fodor's Travel, 2010.

Michelin. *The Green Guide: Languedoc Roussillon Tarn Gorges*. Watford Herts, England: Michelin Travel Publications, 2010.

Williams, Nicola, and Miles Roddis. *Languedoc-Roussillon*. Oakland, CA: Lonely Planet Publications, 2009.

ACKNOWLEDGMENTS

The idea for this book came to me many years ago when I came across an article from the former curator of the Musée d'Art Moderne in Céret, Joséphine Matamoros, who described with great passion the link between the three art movements, Fauvism, Cubism, and Surrealism, and the inspiring landscape of French and Spanish Catalonia. There was a story to explore, and as the years passed, the revelations became more and more fascinating.

I would not have been able to write this book without the help of my dedicated researchers and dear parents, Suzy and Jean-Pierre Raguenaud. The three of us crisscrossed Catalonia, stopping at museums and independent bookstores and buying everything under the sun, including an old book written by Henri Matisse's hairdresser! I deeply appreciate the commitment and enthusiasm they provided for me when I needed a boost.

Thank you to Trish O'Hare for taking on this project and supporting me through the unexpected twists and turns along the way. I have been grateful for her guidance, her kindness, and her generous spirit throughout the writing process.

Thank you to my editor, Jennifer Sale, for her keen eye and most valuable insights.

Acknowledgments

I'm grateful to Marc Latham for allowing me to read through his great-grandfather George-Daniel de Monfreid's still-unpublished personal journals. As a researcher, I tried to focus on the personal letters, diaries, and autobiographies to reveal the stories of these artists, and reading through this particular journal was the highlight of that process. Thank you to Mr. Latham for opening his home to me so generously during my stay. I also would like to thank Antoine Fayet and Magali Rougeot for the memorable visit to the Musée Gustave Fayet at the Abbey of Fontfroide.

Thank you to Elana Rabinowitz, Roni Richey, Diane Adair, and Katherine Holton for their honest feedback and treasured friendship. And to my husband, Vern, thank you for building me my very own writer's studio overlooking the forest and sharing my passion for travel.

ABOUT THE AUTHOR

Virginie Raguenaud was born and raised in France. She spent her childhood summers in Collioure, French Catalonia, where her family has owned property for more than four decades. At the age of twelve, she moved with her parents and two sisters from France to Westfield, New Jersey. Virginie relocated to Montreal to attend McGill University and then finished her bachelor's degree at the Pushkin Institute in Moscow. She identifies herself as a global nomad, raising her own two girls to love travel and art as much as she does. Virginie's first book, *Bilingual By Choice: Raising Kids in Two (or More!) Languages*, was published in 2009.

CPSIA information can be obtained at www.ICGtesting.com
Printed in the USA
BVOW071606270812

298816BV00001B/7/P